AF291499

LIEKO SHIGA

The Tate Photography Series is a celebration of photography by artists in the Tate collection, presenting some of the most significant photographers in the world today. Each book focuses on an individual photographer and includes a specially selected sequence of images and an introduction by a Tate curator, alongside a conversation about each photographer's practice. These collaborations between artists and experts serve to enrich our understanding of photography and its connection to everyday life.

Each year the Tate Photography Series adopts a unifying theme across four books that addresses social, political and cultural issues of our time. The theme for Series Two is Ecology and Environment, featuring photographers who examine aspects of our relationship with the natural world, environment and changing climate.

While overwhelming hard scientific evidence seems all too easy to dispute and ignore, artistic approaches to considering our place in the world appear to be a more effective way to reconnect and change. Photographic artists, ever-curious, sensitive and attuned to noticing patterns, creatively document and mediate reality to help us see.

This series explores Richard Mosse's work in the Amazon rainforest, finding new ways to represent climate change; Chris Killip's Seacoal series in North-East England, where a community subsists on discarded fossil fuel; Lieko Shiga's series *Spiral Shore*, which documents and reimagines a coastal community in Japan's Miyagi Prefecture that was struck by the earthquake and tsunami of 2011; and Claudia Andujar's life work protecting the Yanomani, one of Brazil's largest indigenous groups.

Series Two

2:1   **CLAUDIA ANDUJAR**
2:2   **CHRIS KILLIP**
2:3   **RICHARD MOSSE**
2:4   **LIEKO SHIGA**

LIEKO SHIGA

Edited by
Jess Baxter

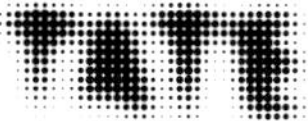

First published 2023 by order of the Tate Trustees
by Tate Publishing, a division of Tate Enterprises Ltd,
Millbank, London SW1P 4RG
www.tate.org.uk/publishing

© Tate Enterprises Ltd 2023
Artworks by Lieko Shiga © Lieko Shiga 2023

All rights reserved. No part of this book may be
reprinted or reproduced or utilised in any form or
by any electronic, mechanical or other means, now
known or hereafter invented, including photocopying
and recording, or in any information storage or
retrieval system, without permission in writing from
the publishers or a licence from the Copyright
Licensing Agency Ltd, www.cla.co.uk

A catalogue record for this book is available from the
British Library

ISBN 978 1 84976 869 6

Distributed in the United States and Canada
by ABRAMS, New York

Library of Congress Control Number applied for

Series Editors: Simon Armstrong and Yasufumi
Nakamori
Senior Editor: Nicola Bion
Production: Bill Jones
Picture Research: Emma O'Neill
Designed by Sarah Boris
Colour reproduction by Westerham Press, London
Printed and bound in the UK by Westerham Press,
London

Front cover: *RASEN KAIGAN 45* 2012 (detail)
Back cover top: *RASEN KAIGAN 45* 2012 (detail)
Back cover bottom: *PIANO 4* 1999

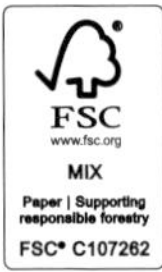

CONTENTS

INTRODUCTION

The photography of Lieko Shiga can be described in many ways: otherworldly, effortless, surreal, poetic. Darkness creeps in from the edge of the photograph, like a dream or part of a map not yet explored. People smile or strange things happen, or both at the same time, like the man who walks through a field with his wife while a leafless tree bursts out of his chest. There's a story within each image, but despite the flash of white-blue light over object and subject, its meaning remains obscured in shadow. The only constant is that we are looking at an earth unlike our own.

Shiga began photographing when she was a teenager. She describes a certain numbness she experienced as a child, when modern life felt too easy, too stifling. She only felt a tremendous surge of energy during dance, which she studied professionally between the ages of seven and sixteen. After playing around with her parents' 35mm film camera, she found that photography soon replaced dance as her obsession. The ability to direct a composition, adjust technical elements and create whole new worlds suddenly alleviated that feeling of not being in control.

Deciding to develop her practice outside of Japan, Shiga studied Fine Art at Chelsea College of Arts in London in the mid-2000s. Here she made *Lilly* 2007, a series of photographic portraits of residents who lived alongside her in East London council flats. The eeriness found in her later work is rooted here, where she draws on exposure techniques from early paranormal photography. Around this time, Shiga created photographs in Brisbane, Singapore and Sendai, which resulted in the publication *CANARY* 2007. It was particularly in Sendai that she felt a strong and visceral connection to the land, as if some ecological spirit had entered her body, and she had become a vessel for the image.

The following winter, when Shiga was driving along the coast of northern Japan, looking for a place to live, she felt another strange and intense calling from the landscape she was passing through. The town was Kitakama, a seemingly insignificant suburb in the quiet region of Miyagi Prefecture. She was immediately struck by the beauty of the ocean, the pine trees and the dusky evening light, and, with great certainty, decided this was the place she had been looking for. She quickly secured a job as the village photographer, and documented the ancient festivals, weddings and funerals that constituted daily life in the community.

But in 2011, everything changed. The town experienced the devastating Tohoku earthquake and tsunami. More than fifty people were killed, and the whole village, including Shiga's home and studio, and the pine trees she so loved, was swept away. Shiga and the villagers stayed in temporary housing while trying to piece together time after the tsunami. Life had changed drastically, but her impulse to photograph did not. Shiga's subsequent work was not the kind of disaster photography you might expect. Instead, Shiga turned her camera to the post-apocalyptic skies, beaches with mysterious tracks and rocks that looked like faces, all glowing with that ethereal camera light.

This resulted in Shiga's hugely celebrated work *RASEN KAIGAN* or *Spiral Shore* 2012, which documented the life of the village before and after the tsunami in equal parts. The interview in this book explores Shiga's time in that community, the work she made during an ecological crisis, and the connection between human spirit and the rhythms of the earth. We talked about how she rescued treasured family photographs from the murky waters of the flood, and how dance remains an important element in her artistic practice.

Seven years after the tsunami, Shiga revisited Miyagi Prefecture to continue her photographic series documenting communities affected by natural disasters. *Human Spring* 2018–19 depicts more people than her earlier work – topless young men loom over the camera, or a farmer with a red-flushed face stares out at us. The Spring in the title evokes a time of renewal, of seasonal change and emergence. There is a sense of hope in the aftermath.

This body of work was at the centre of Shiga's major exhibition at Tokyo Photographic Art Museum in 2019. Since then, Shiga has continued to create work about the northern Japanese landscape – its rocks, maps, trees, roots, soils – and how society is dealing with the aftermath of ecological turmoil, which we will experience increasingly in the coming years. Lieko Shiga's photography continues to capture not only the outside world, but the imaginations and mythologies of our inner worlds too.

Jess Baxter
Assistant Curator, International Art, Tate Modern

JB   When did you first find photography?

LS   I started photographing when I was sixteen years old. Before that time, I had been studying dance at a very serious level. I grew up in Okazaki City, Aichi Prefecture, a place famous for its machinery and manufacturing. Life for me was very clean and convenient and safe. But this made my body feel very uncomfortable. The automatic nature of modern life meant I couldn't feel anything. That's why it felt so good to dance – when I danced, I became breathless, I could experience physical sensation, and everything in my body started to make sense.

But as a teenager, my body changed. I wasn't so happy when I danced anymore. It was at this time that I found photography. After taking some photographs at the High School Athletic Festival with my parents' automatic compact camera. I had a little 35mm film left, so I took some photos of the items that I had arranged on my desk. I just did it unconsciously. I thought, 'maybe I can change and control this everyday life, if I use this small old camera'. That kind of thought felt awful and dangerous. But it also felt really comfortable to me, and from there I fell in love with photography.

JB   You studied Fine Art at Chelsea College of Arts in London. Could you tell me a bit about what sort of work you created there?

LS   I went to university in Japan once, but the photography programme there was too focused on creating advertisements or finding the right lighting. My photography is more focused on creating something; on the relationship between myself and society. So I went to Chelsea College of Arts, and it was really, really good for me. The course taught you philosophy, more about the world. Artists came to the school to give talks – my tutor was Georgina Starr, a video artist associated with the Young British Artists of the early 1990s. It was so helpful to learn from her, she was really kind.

JB   Was it something she said?

LS   I just really enjoyed her talk; it was very different from a Japanese university teacher. We had a chat about what we were working on. That kind of natural conversation really helped me, and her concept inspired me to create work from everyday life.

JB   You made the series *Lilly* while living in East London. How did that body of work come about?

LS   I made a little black box in the street near my apartment. I stood in front of it and invited people to have their photograph taken inside. I can't really do that nowadays – it would be too mysterious or strange. I was this little Japanese girl, and I called to anyone who passed by 'Hi, I'm studying photography, can I take your photograph?' Most of the people said yes. My approach to people was like the training I had in dancing; it was like choreography. I always had a conversation with the person, I asked many questions. People would talk about their memories or their sadness, and I asked them to think about these memories when I took the photograph. I wanted to make them into a totally fictional person in my work.

JB   It sounds like the relationship and connection you establish with people you photograph is really important to your process. You approached people in a similar way when you moved to Kitakama several years later. Can you tell me a bit about that?

LS   From that experience, I learned that my camera can be a communication tool. In 2008, I decided to move to Kitakama

Village. Japan is a very long island, and I grew up in the centre, so I had never really seen northern Japan before. The first time I went there, I was really surprised by the landscape. It was so emotional for me, it was so beautiful. I couldn't believe it was in Japan.

I was still trying to learn about the world. Even if I took thousands or millions of photographs, I still didn't know what I was photographing. I didn't know the name of that mountain, I didn't know the name of this rock and so on. That's why I moved to Kitakama – I had to get inside that image to take a photograph. I had to live there to understand.

I started to record the oral history from the elderly people, speaking to each person for hours or days. Of course I had studied the history of Japan, but really, I didn't know anything. I didn't know about the Second World War or the lives of older women. This experience changed my life.

JB What sort of things did they tell you?

LS Everybody had grown up in the village, so the environment was the same, but the stories people were telling me were completely different. There was so much diversity in their memories. Often the stories were oo private, I couldn't record them in official village records. Even their families didn't know.

I think for them it felt safe to talk about these stories because I was an outsider, an alien. When I asked to take their photograph, I would say to the person that they were like an actor or actress in front of my camera: 'You are a totally different person here, so please feel safe.' I felt like the private story was on my body, and I had to spend time creating a new story out of the old. That was the *Spiral Shore* project.

JB It sounds like they really trusted you, like the people in your black box in London. How did life change for you and the villagers with the tsunami?

LS I had been dreaming about creating a performance or theatre programme for the villagers. I thought it would be a nice thing to do for the community, with my background in dancing. But then the earthquake and the tsunami came, and my village was totally destroyed.

We lost more than fifty people from the village at one time. I remember that night – it was very dark, snowing, so cold, and we had no idea how many people had died. Everything stopped. Everything was in the water. I remember thinking 'I should remember this moment'. I thought back to how I felt as a child, that everyday life was convenient but uncomfortable. But now I knew this to be the real world. I felt very real.

We started a very busy life in the shelter. We stayed there for three months, and then we were moved to temporary housing for three years. I had lost my camera in the tsunami, so I borrowed one from my friends, and I started taking photographs again.

Then photographs from everyone's homes started washing up. There were so many. Because I had listened to so many private stories, and had got to know the townspeople, I knew everyone's faces.

JB   Photographs you found? In the floods from the tsunami?

LS   Yes, photographs were everywhere. Photographic paper is very light and resilient in water, so many survived. But because the tsunami was saltwater, over the months the images slowly began disappearing. So I decided to collect and clean them up. I gave them back to the people they belonged to. You have to remember that this kind of activity was happening all along the east coast of Japan. But my village had 100 families there, so me and my friends wanted to help.

The photos were really damaged, so we digitised them, burned them to DVD and returned them to their owners. It was a really important experience for me. I hung the photographs on the wall to dry out, and then everybody looked for their own photograph. It was like a photographic installation. Not an exhibition – but a space used for photography. So many snapshots. So many memories.

I remember one story. One old lady was trying to look for her daughter's photograph. Her daughter had been killed in the tsunami. Finally, she found it. Suddenly that photograph took on the meaning of her daughter's very body. She reacted so strongly. It wasn't just paper anymore – the photograph was the body itself. But on the other side from that, another lady picked up a photo of a family member, and just threw it away. I noticed then that the photographic paper could mean just a piece of paper, like trash, or become like an actual human body. The meaning could be so different. That experience was really heavy for me. A photograph can be anything.

JB   I'm sorry you experienced this. It was some time ago now, but it must be really painful to talk about still.

LS   No, it's OK, don't worry. We had the funerals, and because I was still the village photographer, I also took the funeral portraits, which was a very important process. The human body disappears but people who are left try to preserve the image.

JB   How did your relationship with nature change after the tsunami hit?

LS   The landscape had totally changed. It's nothing now. Before the tsunami there was a beautiful pine forest and houses. But after the tsunami, trash was everywhere. When the government cleaned up everything, it was just the ground and the sky. Of course, people's souls are left. This is why I continued to take photographs in the shelter and temporary housing. Half of the photographs in *Spiral Shore* are before, and half are taken after the tsunami. It's amazing. Nobody notices which is which.

JB   Yes, I really noticed that. It's not so much a series about the tsunami, it's about the people and the land. A lot of your photography shows natural processes in which you have intervened – like the beach where you made markings in the sand with an old tree, or the photograph with a watermelon under someone's T-shirt. I get the sense that you try to regain agency over nature at times when nature feels uncontrollable.

LS   Yes, for example there are many photographs of rocks painted white in that series. Because the landscape was gone, I was looking down at the ground when I was walking through the village – I couldn't find anything to photograph. Suddenly I started taking photographs of stones – from little pieces of sand, to big rocks. I started to paint them white, like a person's face in a funeral portrait. Then I used a strong flash light for each stone. I wasn't sure what I was doing!

But I suddenly noticed that each stone looked like a human face. Or a rock looked like a mountain. Or maybe it looked like anything at all. I showed these many white stones to the village people, and everyone started reading unique stories from the stones' images. I understood then that people can look at the photograph like a mirror of their own heart. If the person is feeling sad in that moment, then they will see something sad or awful in the photograph. The image reflects the image. That's at the end of *Spiral Shore*.

JB   Your later series *Human Spring* includes some images of your friend known as S-chan, a Kitakama farmer. He had developed a mental health condition that meant he was deeply affected by the season of spring, and he would experience intense physical and mental changes. There's an interesting comparison to farmers in the UK, who have some of the highest rates of poor mental health in the country. For lots of reasons, I think there are parallels. How do you think mental health is tied to the land?

LS   It's quite difficult to explain S-chan. He had bipolar disorder. It was caused by shock – one day he found all his vegetables had died, after trying new modern farming processes. For him, it was not the natural way to grow crops. Because I am a modern person, I cannot understand what this shock was like for him, so I don't know about this powerful connection to nature. But S-chan – he grew up in a completely natural way of life. He was part of nature. That's why he experienced a mental illness from using the modern way.

I remember the first moment I encountered northern Japanese nature. I felt really emotional. It felt so real. There was a strange secret to why I felt it was so beautiful. Maybe he knew this secret too. So I'm still looking for that level of feeling, but I will not be able to feel it like he did.

JB   I think we can learn from people like that, this reverence towards nature and taking care of the planet. I read somewhere that because you don't know the final image when you're shooting, you try to 'call the spirit' from the land into the photograph.

LS   Yes, I use the camera to feel the world which I cannot see with my naked eye. It connects to the spirit and goes into the photograph. The camera is just an empty box with a mirror in it. That mirror is very important. It's why I painted the stones white – it explored this idea of the image being a mirror. People see what they want to see.

JB   Is that something you want for people who encounter your photographs for the first time? To make up their own meaning, bring their own story to it?

LS   Yes – it's really different from something like video work. Photography is just a few seconds. Like one breath. I really like that aspect. I can see with just one breath.

Maybe you can find unique time and space in my documents. Photography is not quite the future or past or present, it is an eternal moment. Because we get closer to death by the second, the body is time itself. This is why we are scared of death, it reminds us that we have a finite amount of time. That's why I really feel in love with creating worlds with a camera.

JB   Capturing the timelessness of the moment, you often use an incredibly bright photo flash. Do you plan for that to happen, or do you edit photographs in post-production?

LS   Except for the work in my current show at the Museum of Contemporary Art Tokyo, I never use Photoshop. For *Spiral Shore*, I adjusted the photographic processes in my lab. I set up the stone flash light with handmade lights. I like bringing out the noise – the bright spots in the dark. Most of the time it is rain or fog. Sometimes I use a flash light to illuminate water droplets to create a theatrical feeling.

JB   This theatrical element certainly gives an air of mystery to your photographs. Do you intend for your pictures to look a bit mysterious or magical, or does that happen by chance?

LS   It's half and half. When I decide to create a work, I plan the situation
        very carefully and strictly in advance. Then I invite the person who I
        will photograph, and we talk for a long time. I am always waiting for
        the moment something unexpected happens. Sometimes it takes
        a few days, or sometimes it happens in a few seconds. I really don't
        know when it's going to happen. If I control everything, that's really
        boring, but I try to prepare as much as I can.

JB   Could you tell me a bit about the presentation of your
        photography? Your installation of *Human Spring* in 2019 showed
        your photography on large light boxes.

LS   The photographic exhibition happens *inside* a space, it's not like
        creating photobooks. You can flick through books anywhere, but
        creating an exhibition ... you walk around the space, you have a
        360-degree sensory experience. We have no idea if a person feels
        something more on one part of the body or another. So I create the
        space not as an installation using photography but instead as a
        photographic space, like you are entering a snapshot. I make little
        sculptures of how I want the space to look – it takes so much time
        to work out the physical space. But of course I like photography
        in a frame too – because a frame is like a coffin. It contains a life
        someone once lived.

JB   What are you working on next?

LS   In some ways, we understand a tsunami because it's nature. It just
        happens. But the reconstruction after the tsunami is really powerful
        for me. I am interested in how society or a company or a nation
        deals with natural events. It is how people control the situation that
        is interesting to me. When I think about these issues, it forces me
        to think about who I am. My existence, where I've come from, what
        I've learned, how I look at the world. I would like to learn more about
        the reconstruction efforts across Japan. It has already been twelve
        years since the tsunami, but the situation has changed drastically
        in northern Japan, especially around Fukushima. Because I am
        in the art world, I can try to tell these stories. It's a really exciting
        period for me, a chance to make workshops, lectures or talks to
        raise awareness about what happened. I will continue to do that.

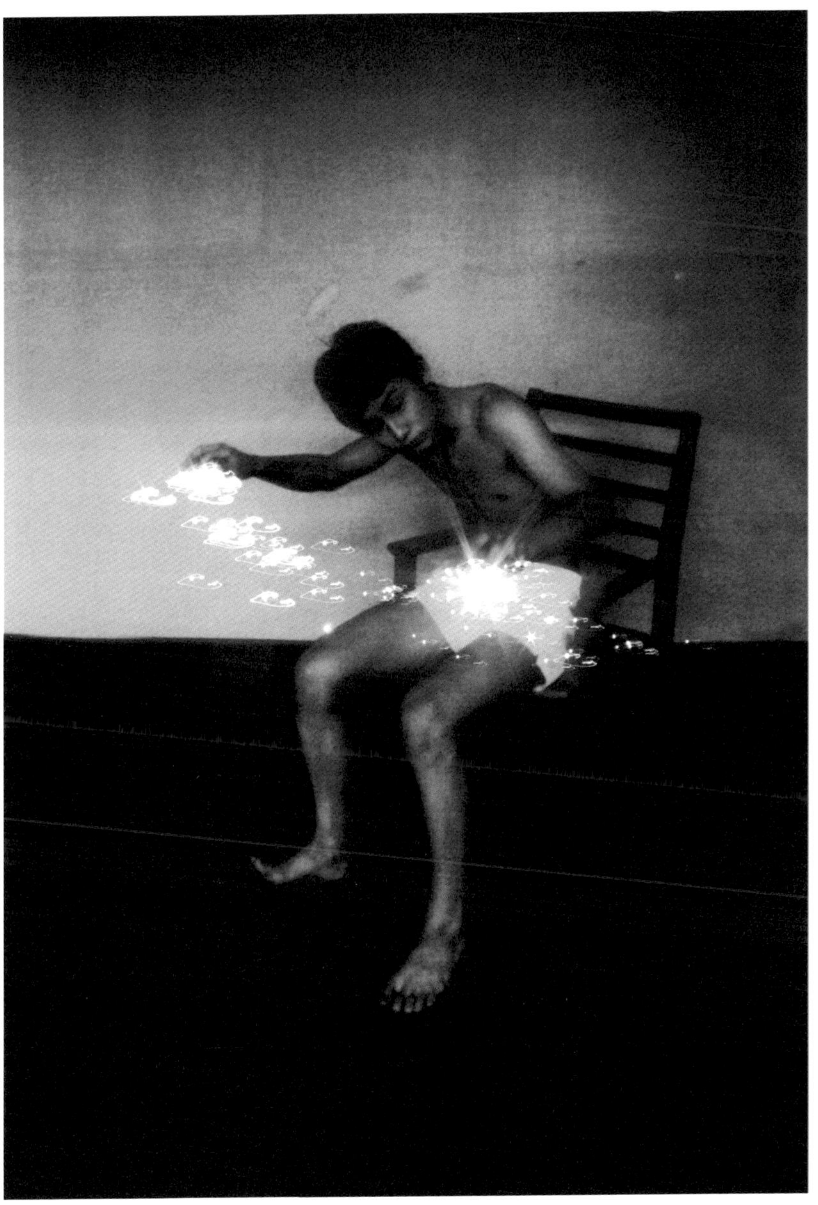

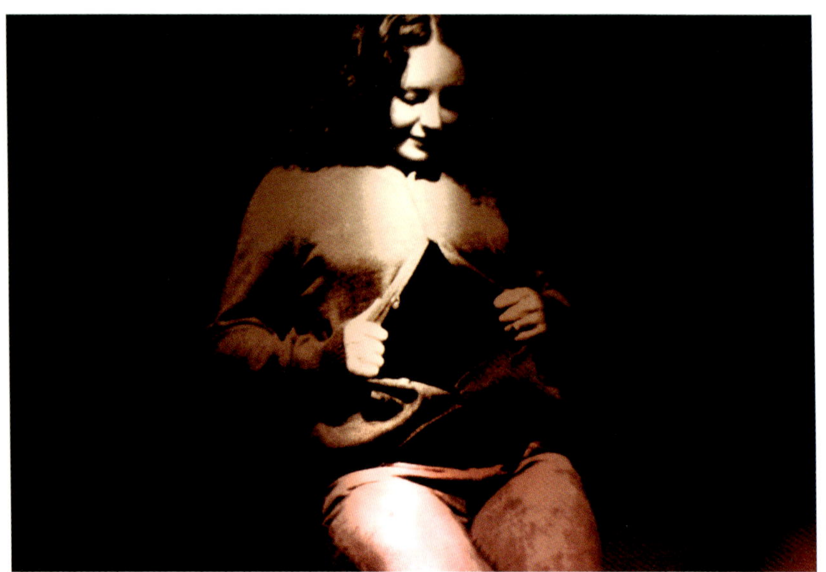

18	*Bethany* 2005 (*Lilly* series)

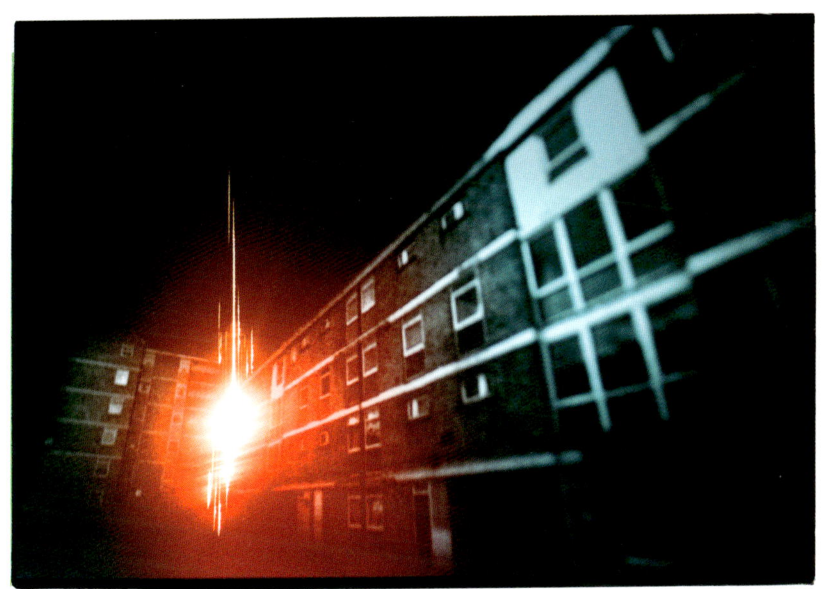

 No.8 Damien Court 2004 (*Lilly* series)

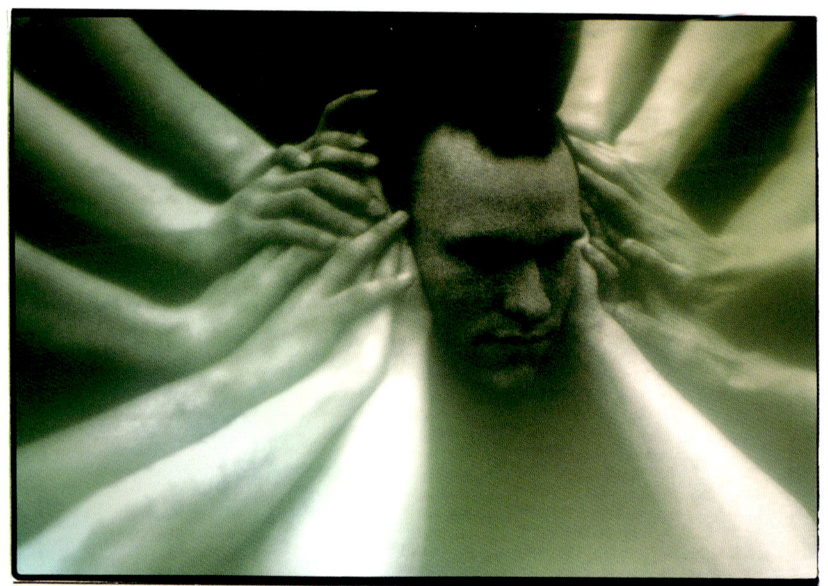

     Tomlinson FC 2005 (*Lilly* series)

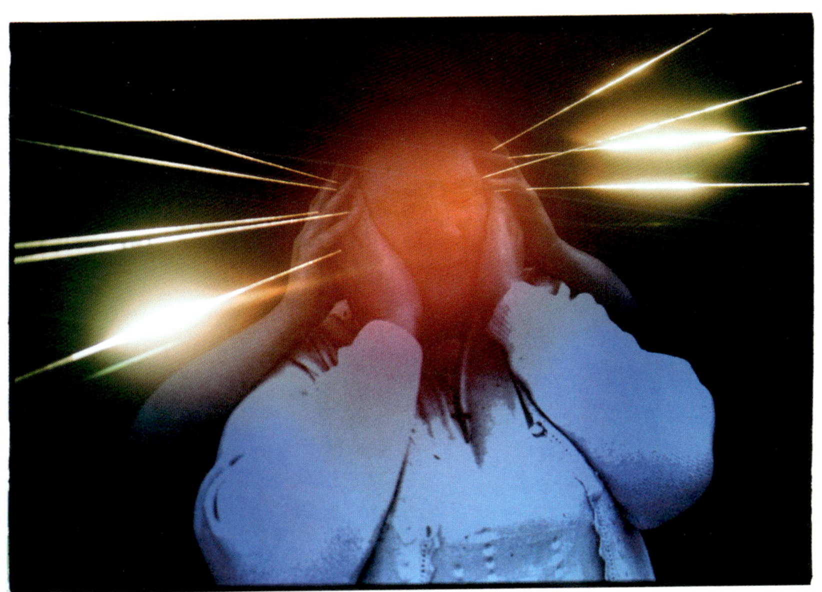

 Jane's shout 2005 (*Lilly* series)

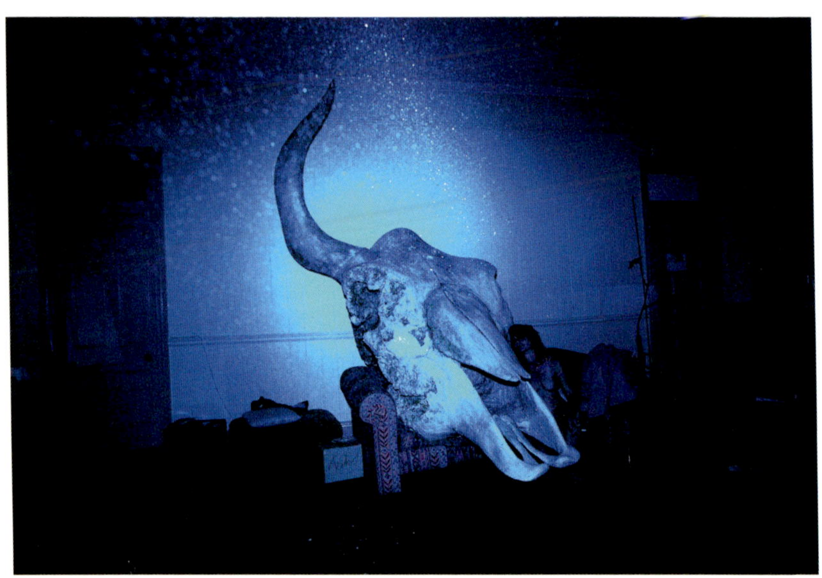

 Out of Eden 2007 (*CANARY* series)

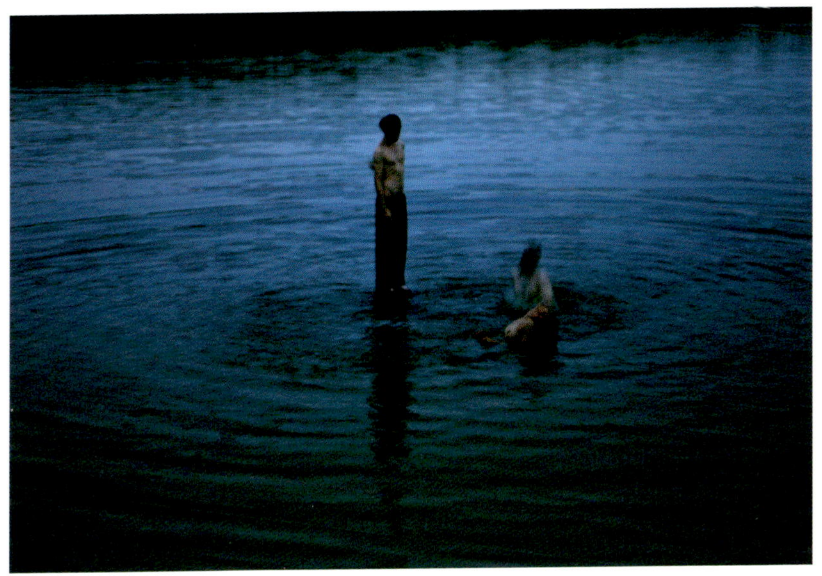

   Dominique 2006 (*CANARY* series)

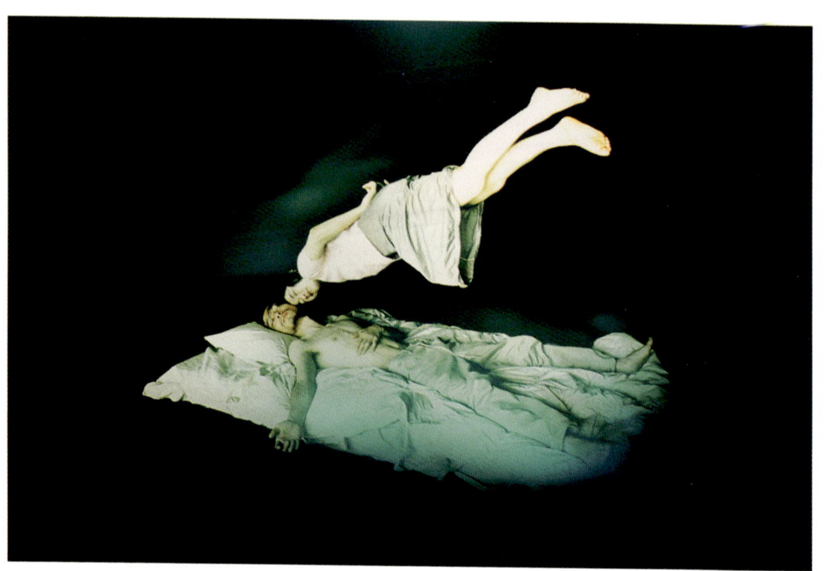

  Chiako 2006 (*CANARY* series)

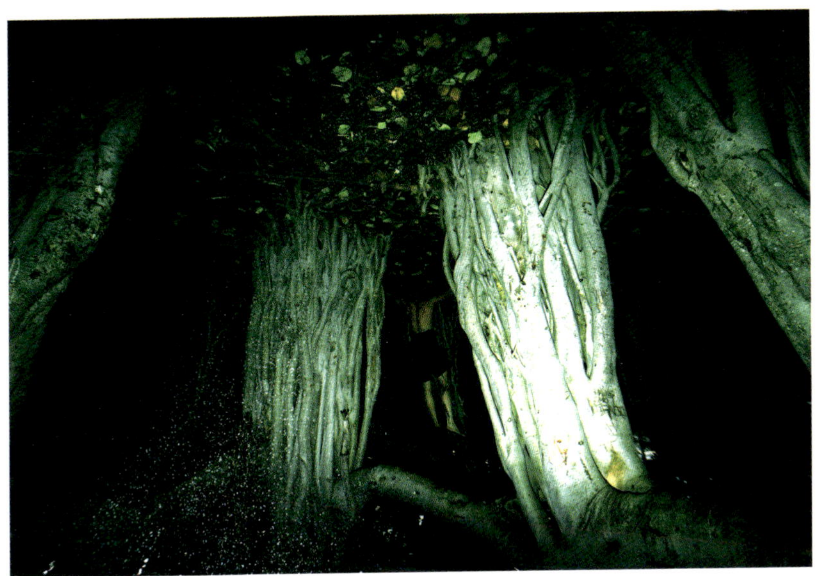

  Forest of Figs 2006 (*CANARY* series)

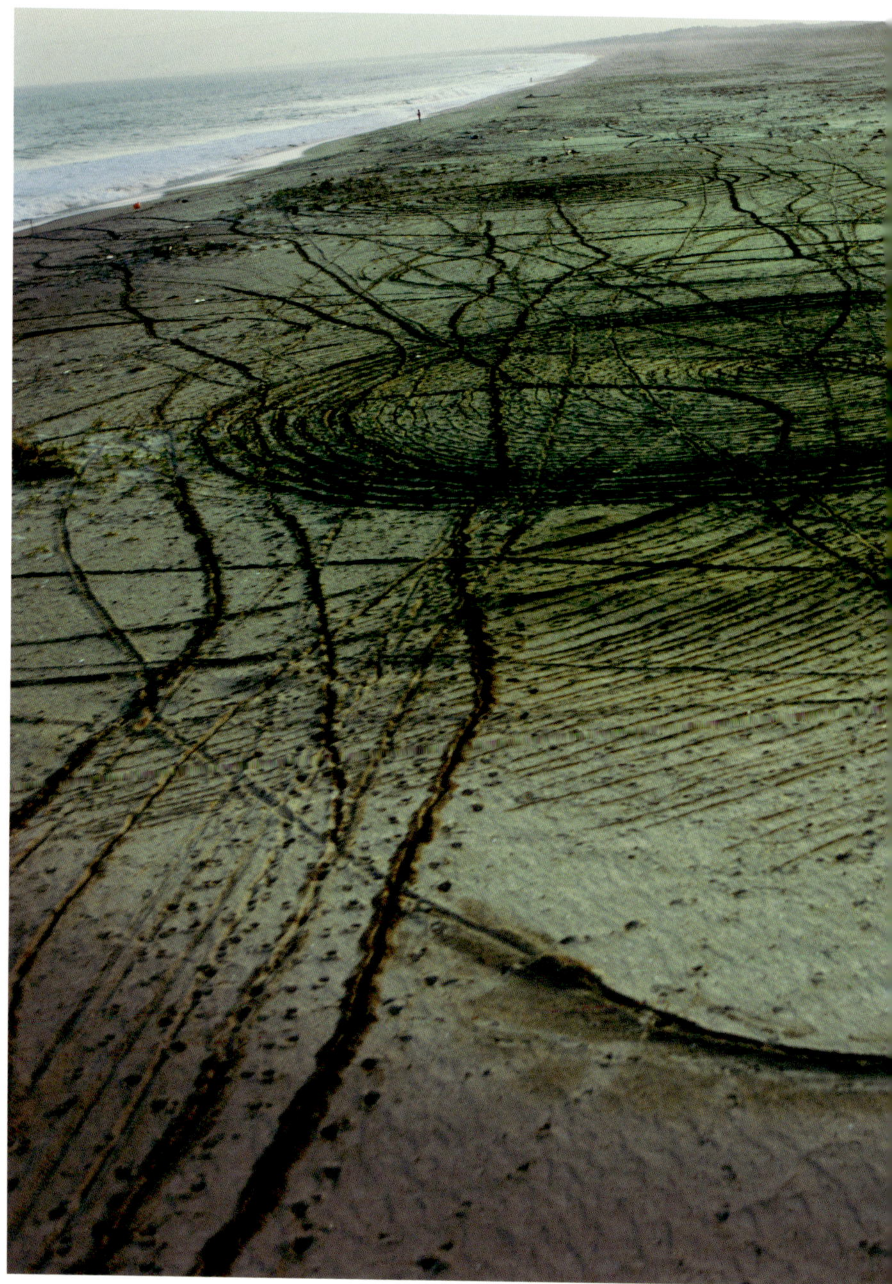

 RASEN KAIGAN 46 (Another Cut) 2012

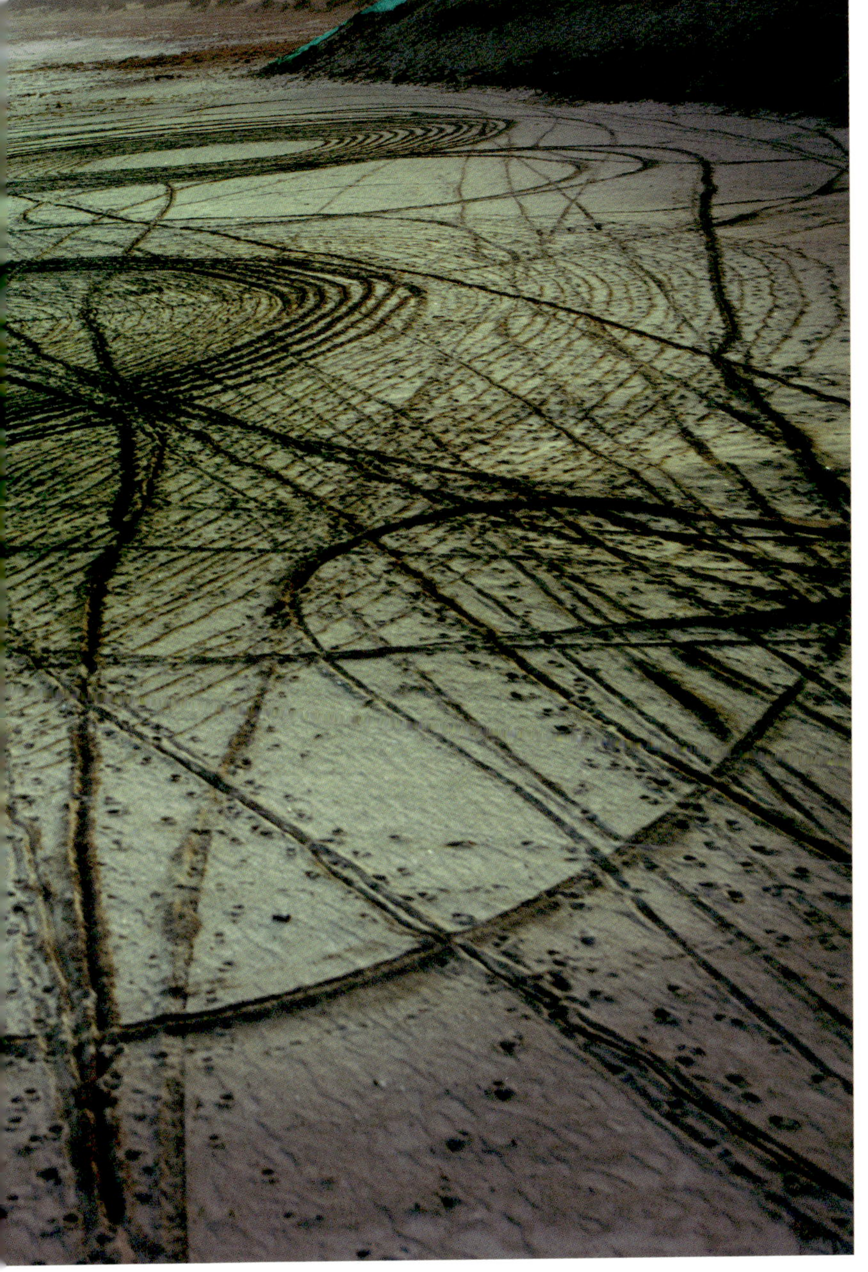

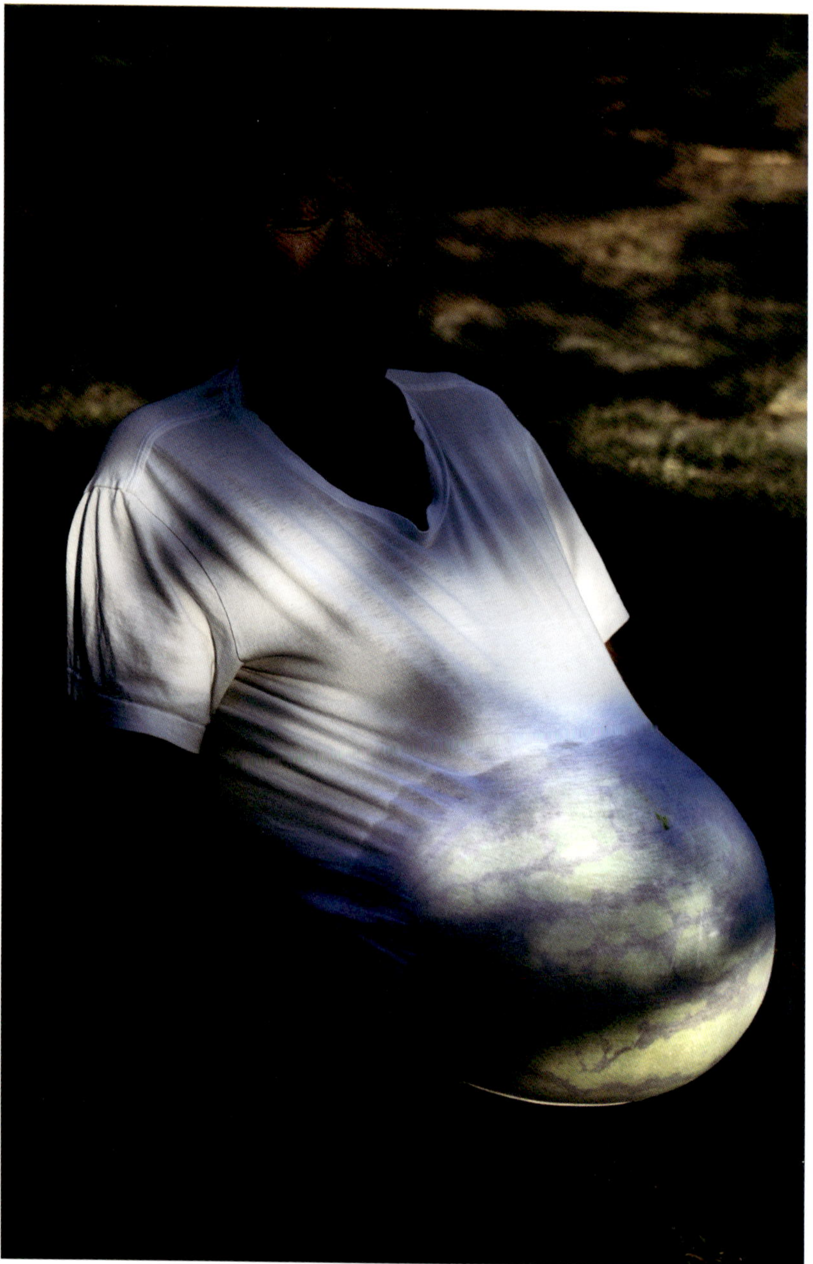

 Meat is Meat, Fish is Fish 2012 (*RASEN KAIGAN* series)

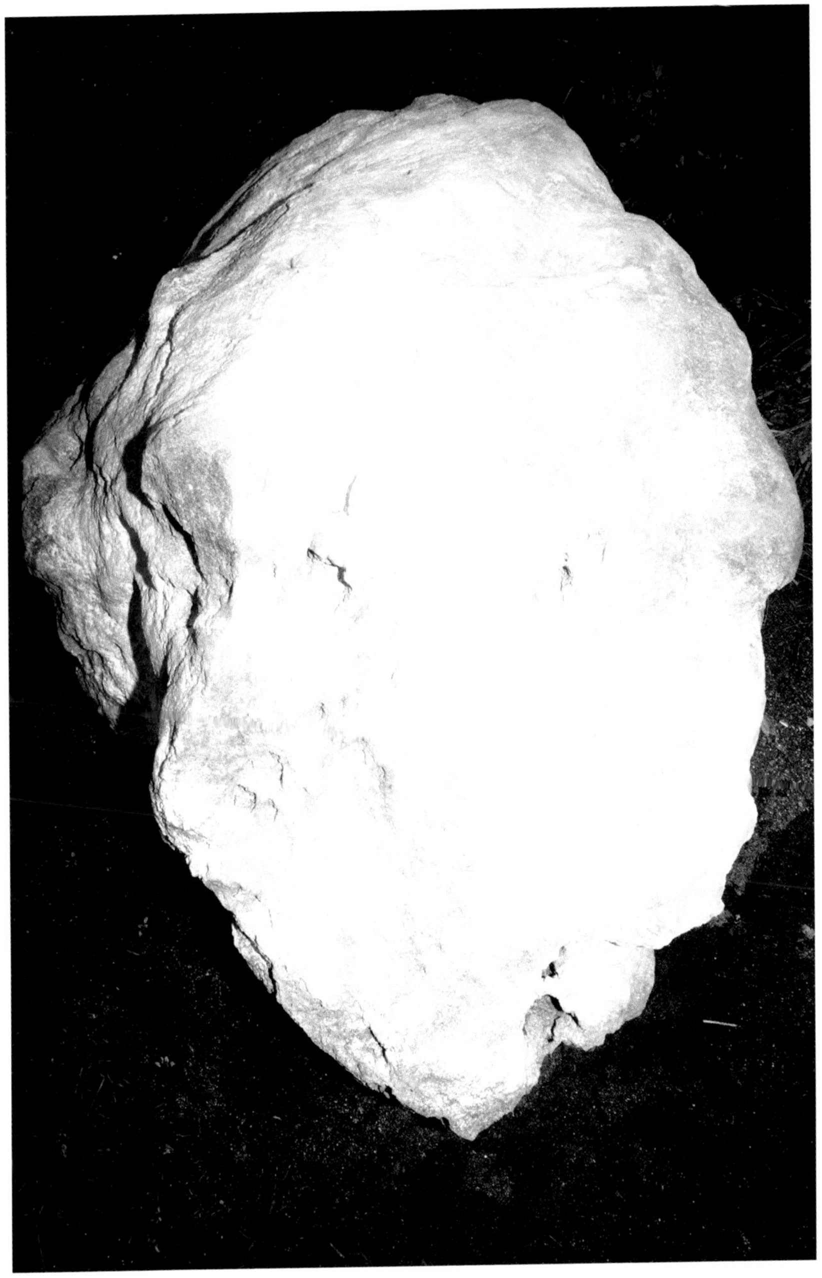

   349243 2012 (*RASEN KAIGAN* series)

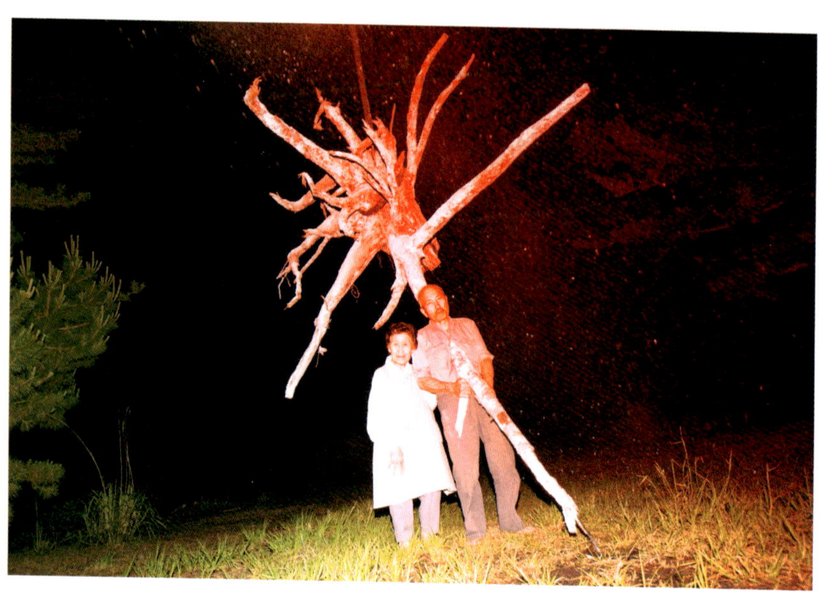

 RASEN KAIGAN 45 2012 (*RASEN KAIGAN* series)

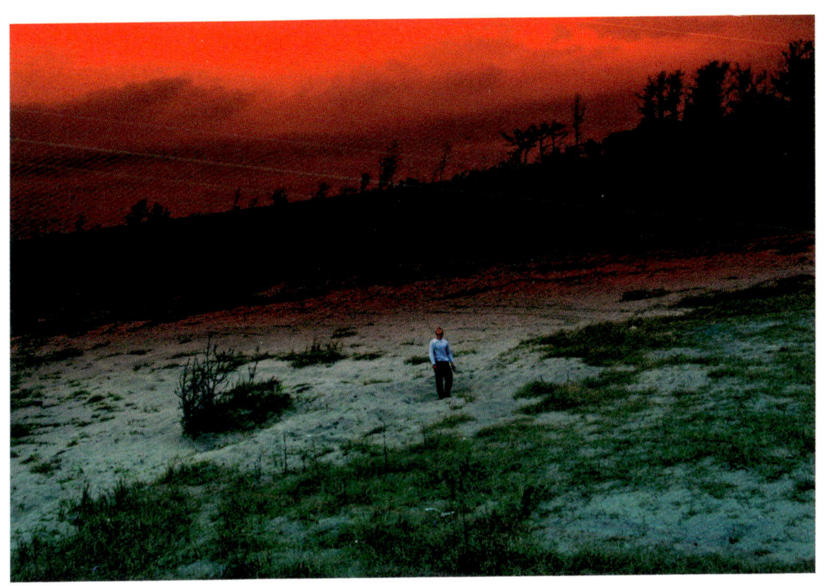

 RASEN KAIGAN 45 2012 (*RASEN KAIGAN* series)

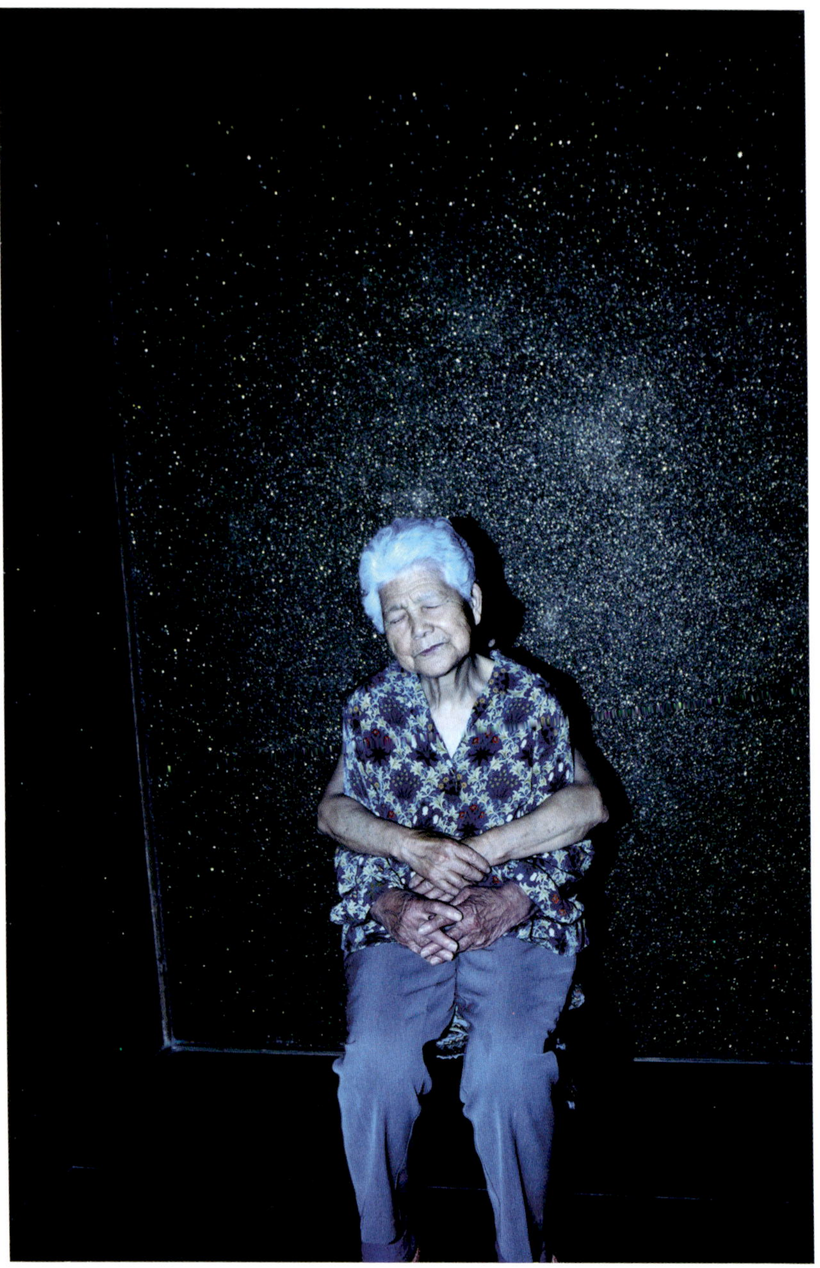

  Mother's Gentle Hands 2012 (*RASEN KAIGAN* series)

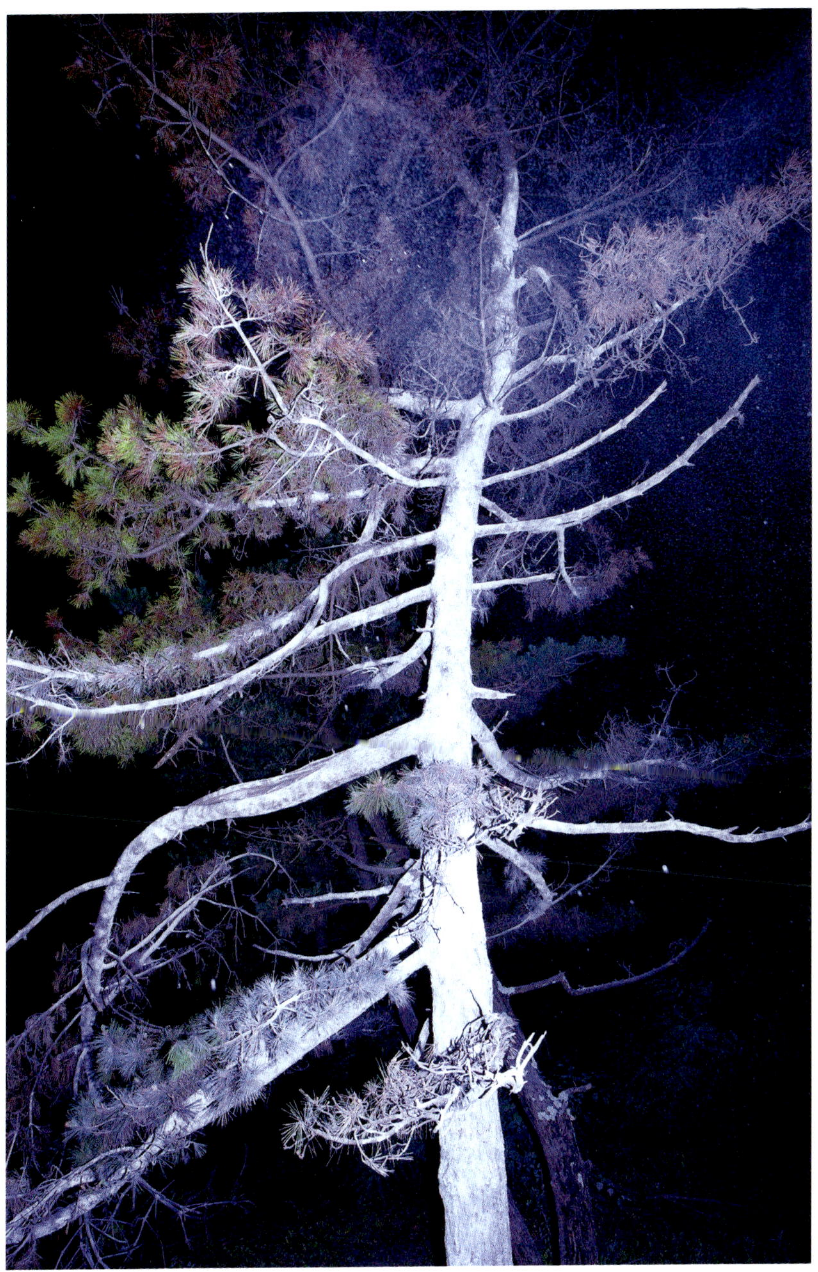

 RASEN KAIGAN 36 2012 (*RASEN KAIGAN* series)

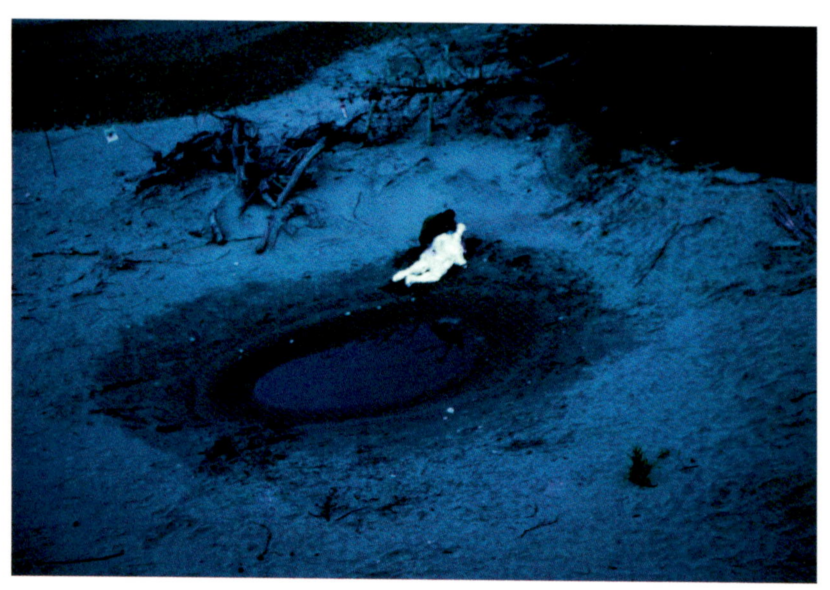

 I was an alien 2012 (*RASEN KAIGAN* series)

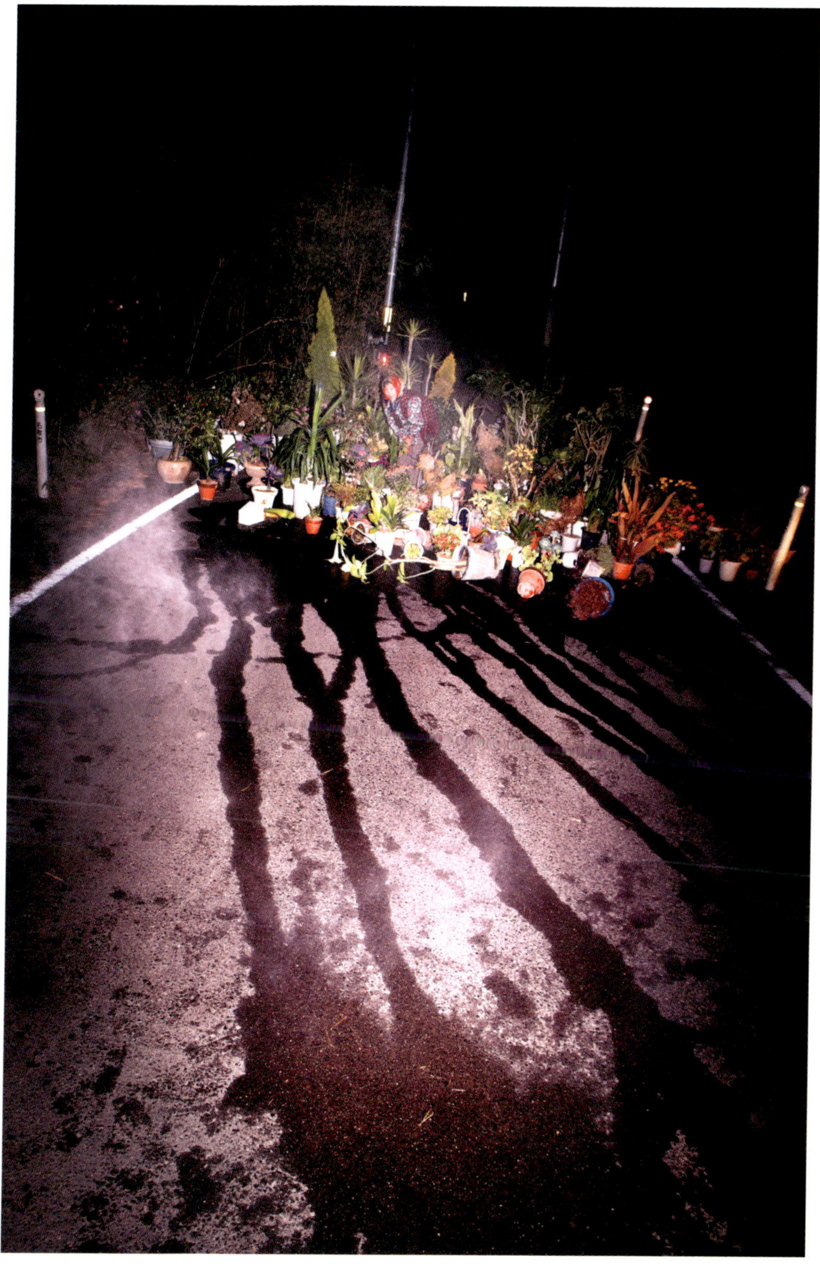

 Garden of tears 2010 (*RASEN KAIGAN* series)

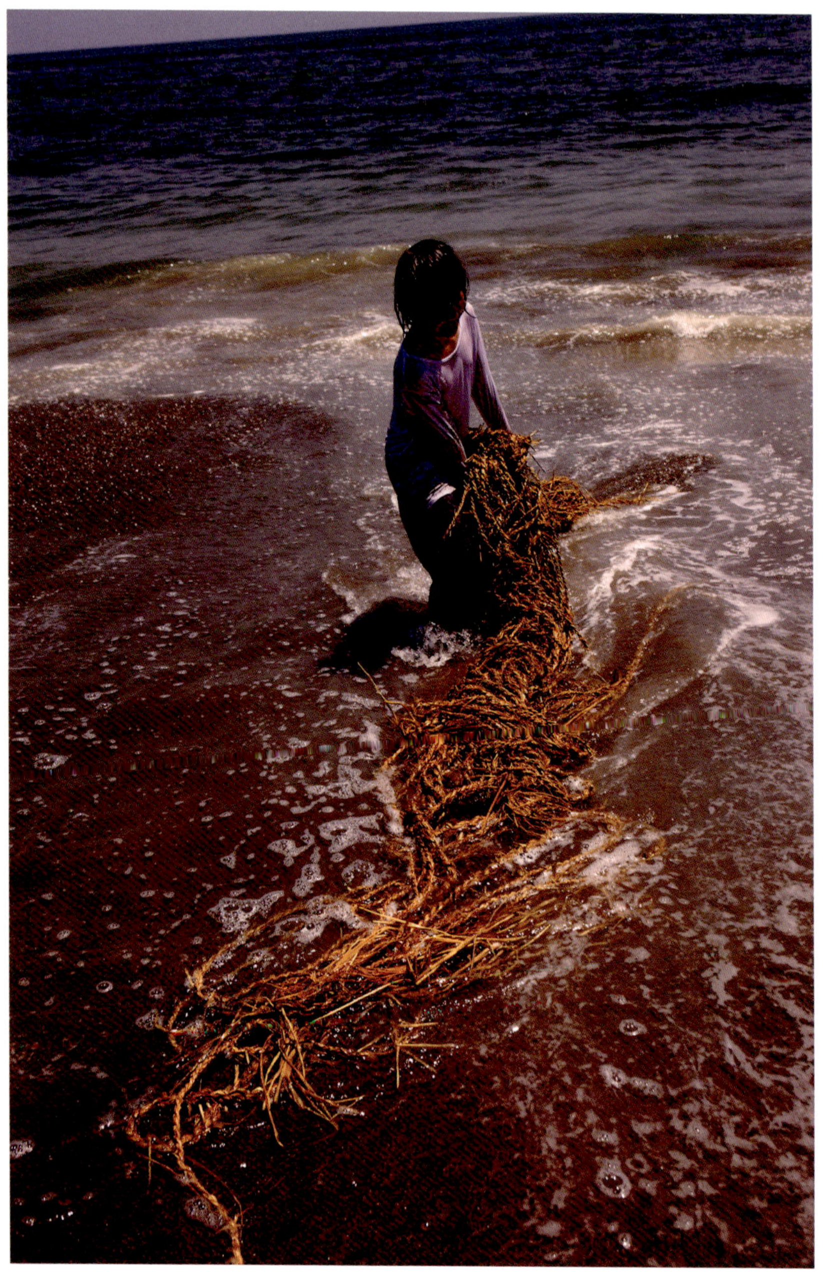

 RASEN KAIGAN 34 2012 (RASEN KAIGAN series)

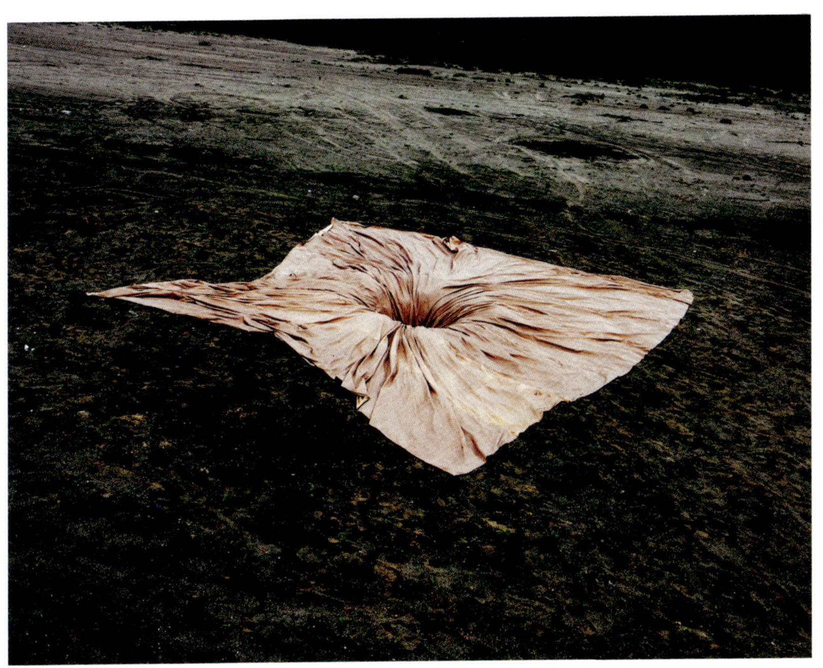

 RASEN KAIGAN 28 2012 (*RASEN KAIGAN* series)

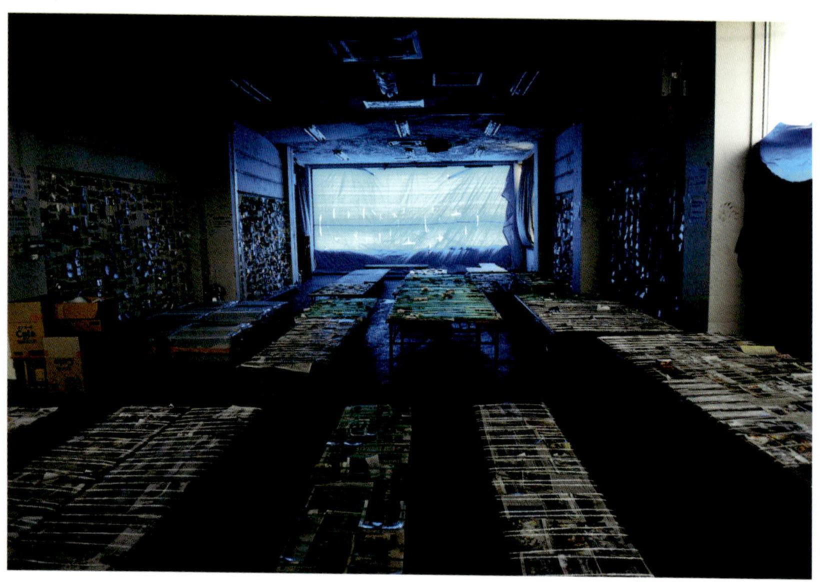

 Katakana assembly house used for cleaning photographs 2012

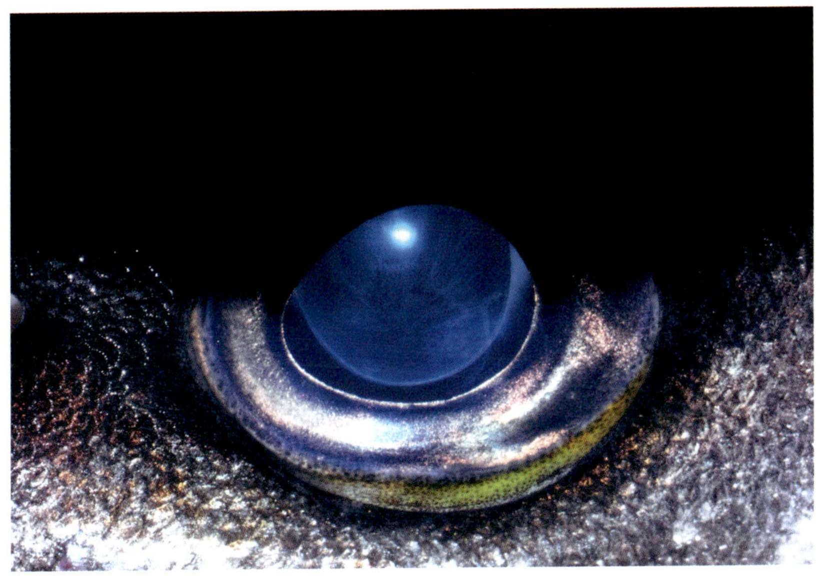

  I lived with a monster 2012 (*RASEN KAIGAN* series)

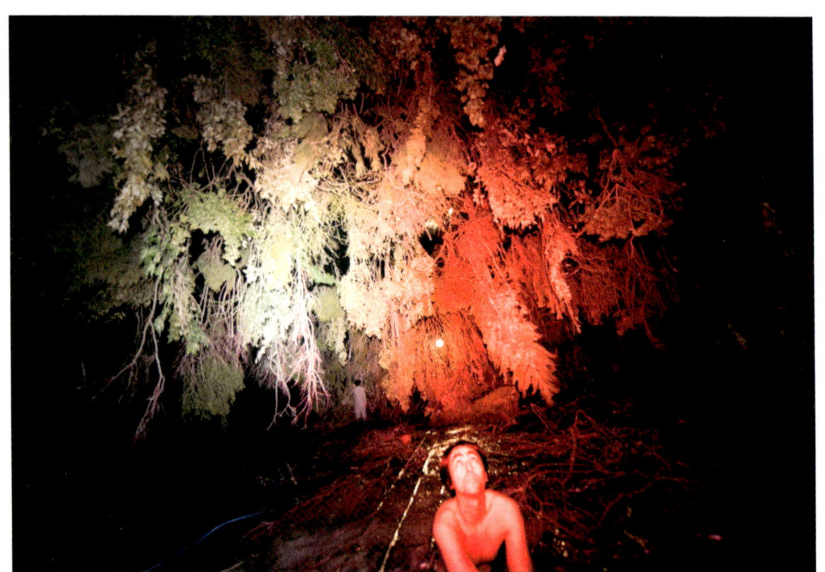

   I can see it in him 2019 (*Human Spring* series)

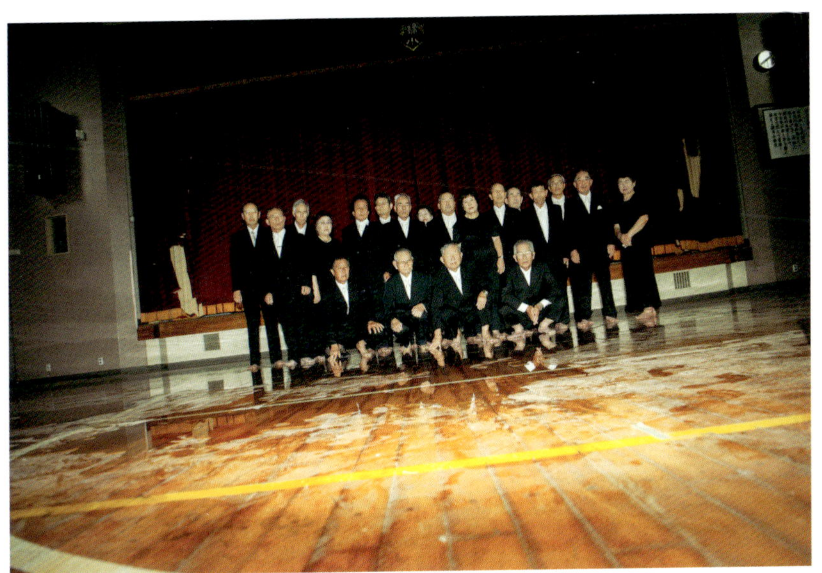

   Lost for songs 2016 (*Human Spring* series)

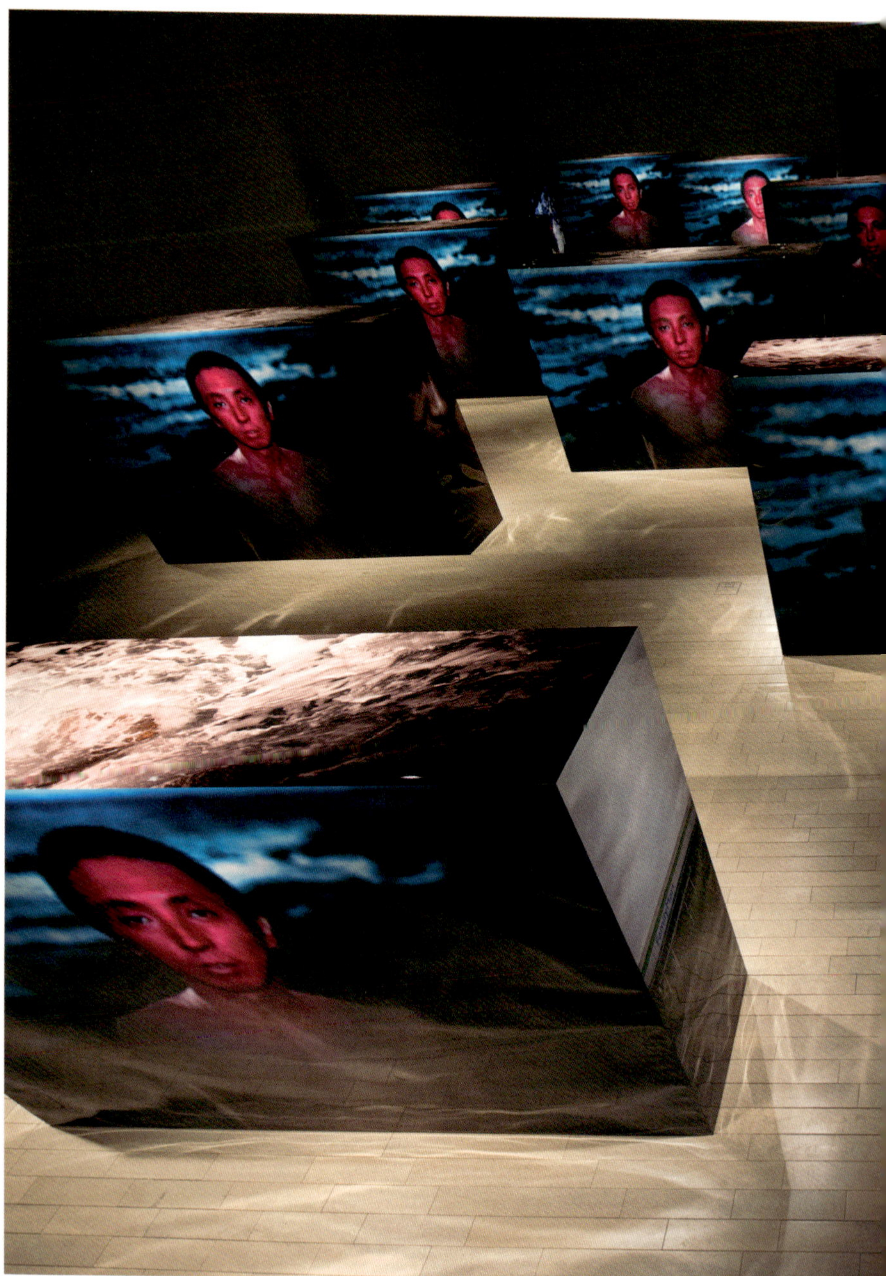

Installation view of *Human Spring*, Tokyo Photographic Art Museum, 2019

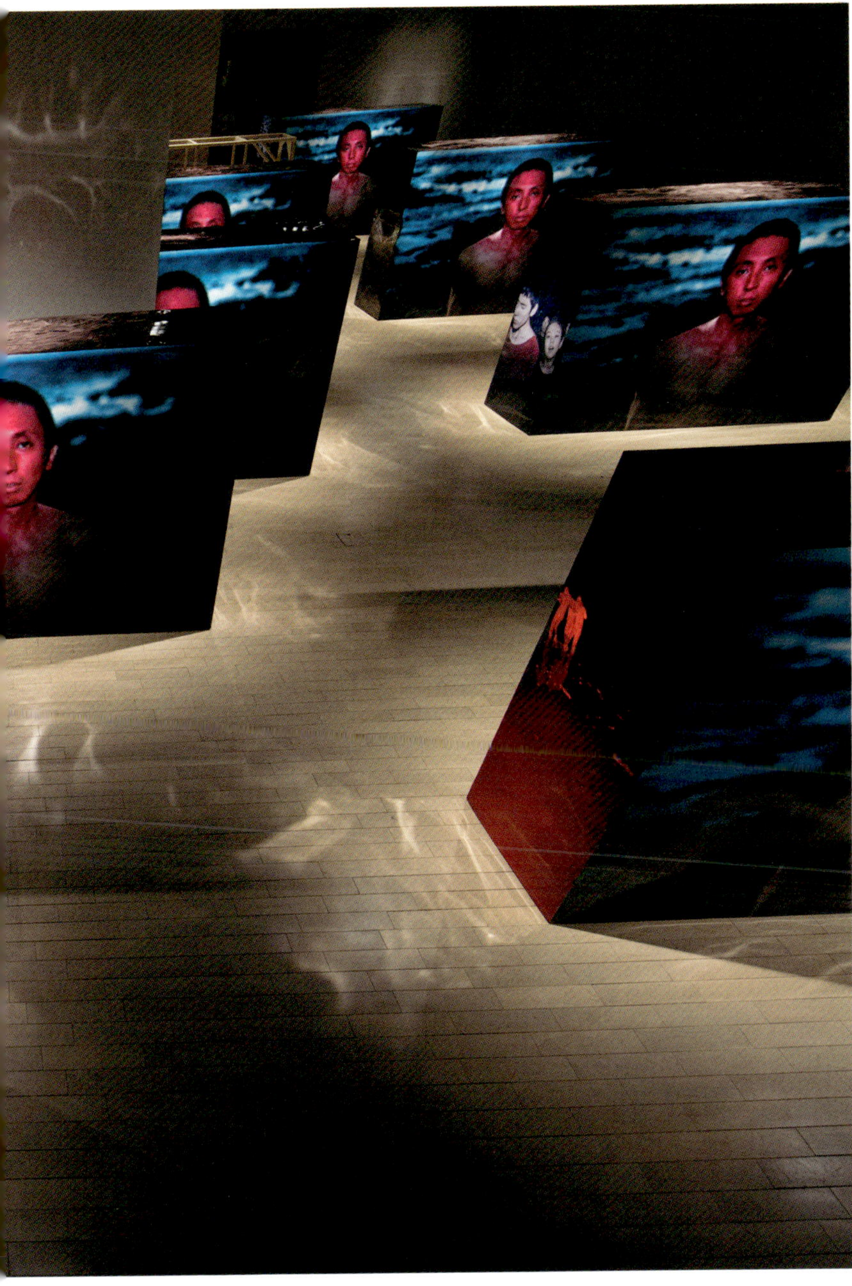

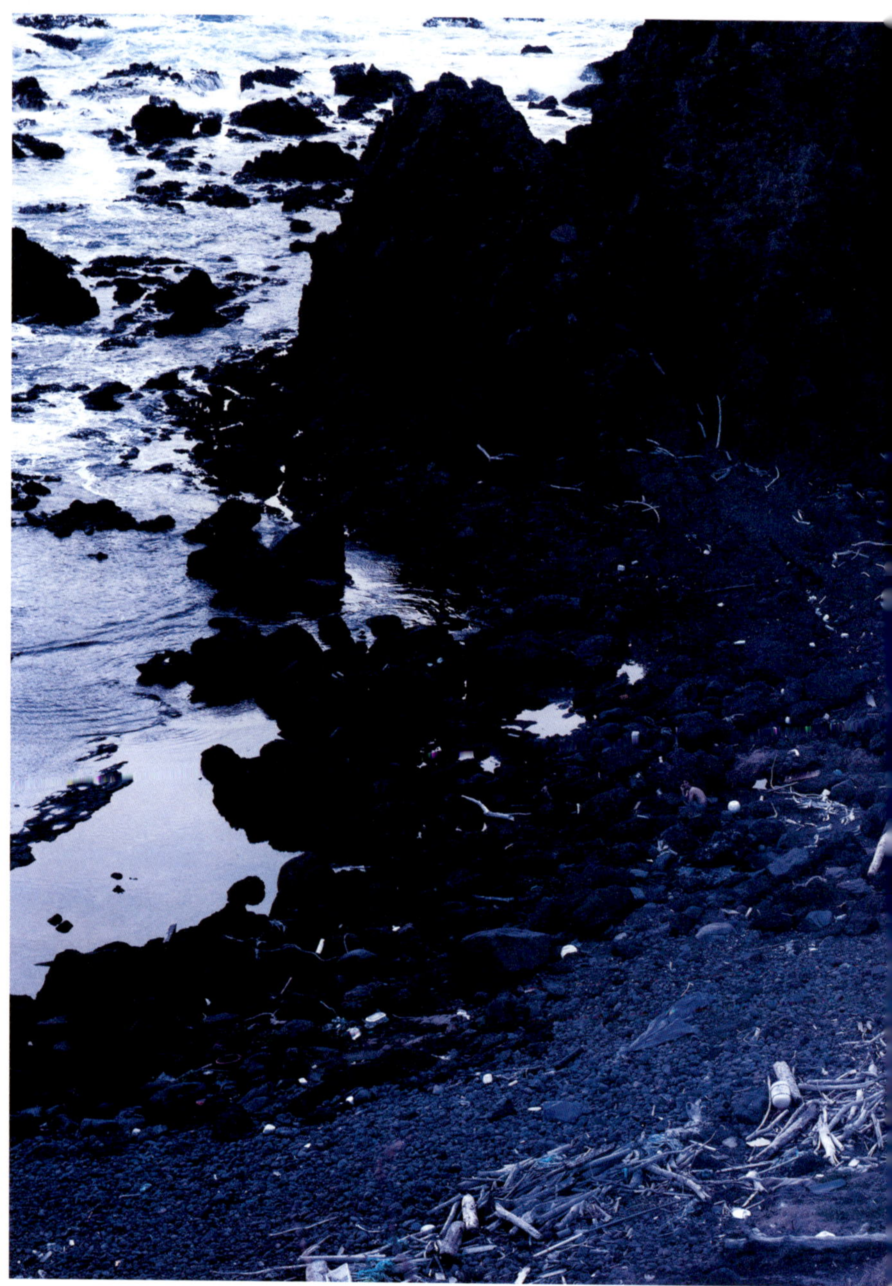

 The Food Chain 2019 (*Human Spring* series)

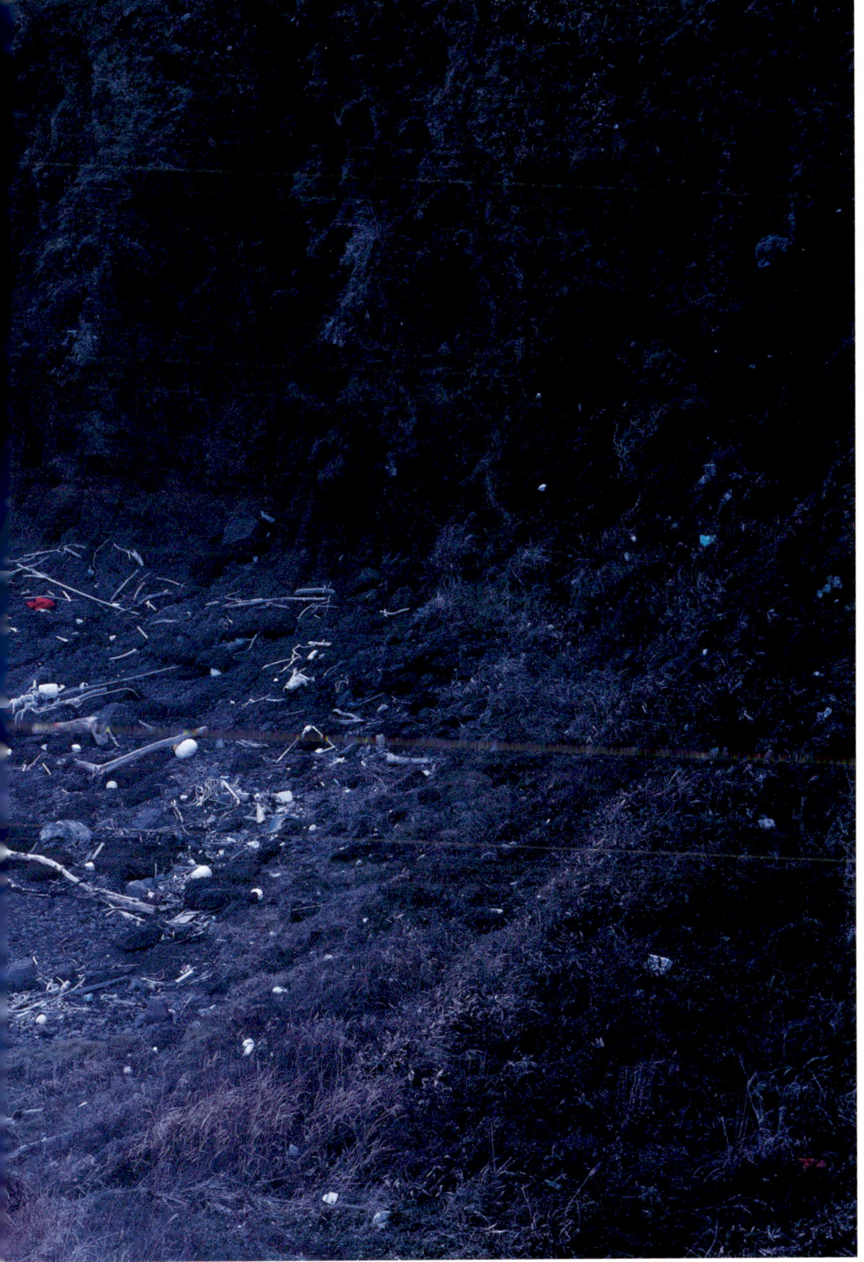

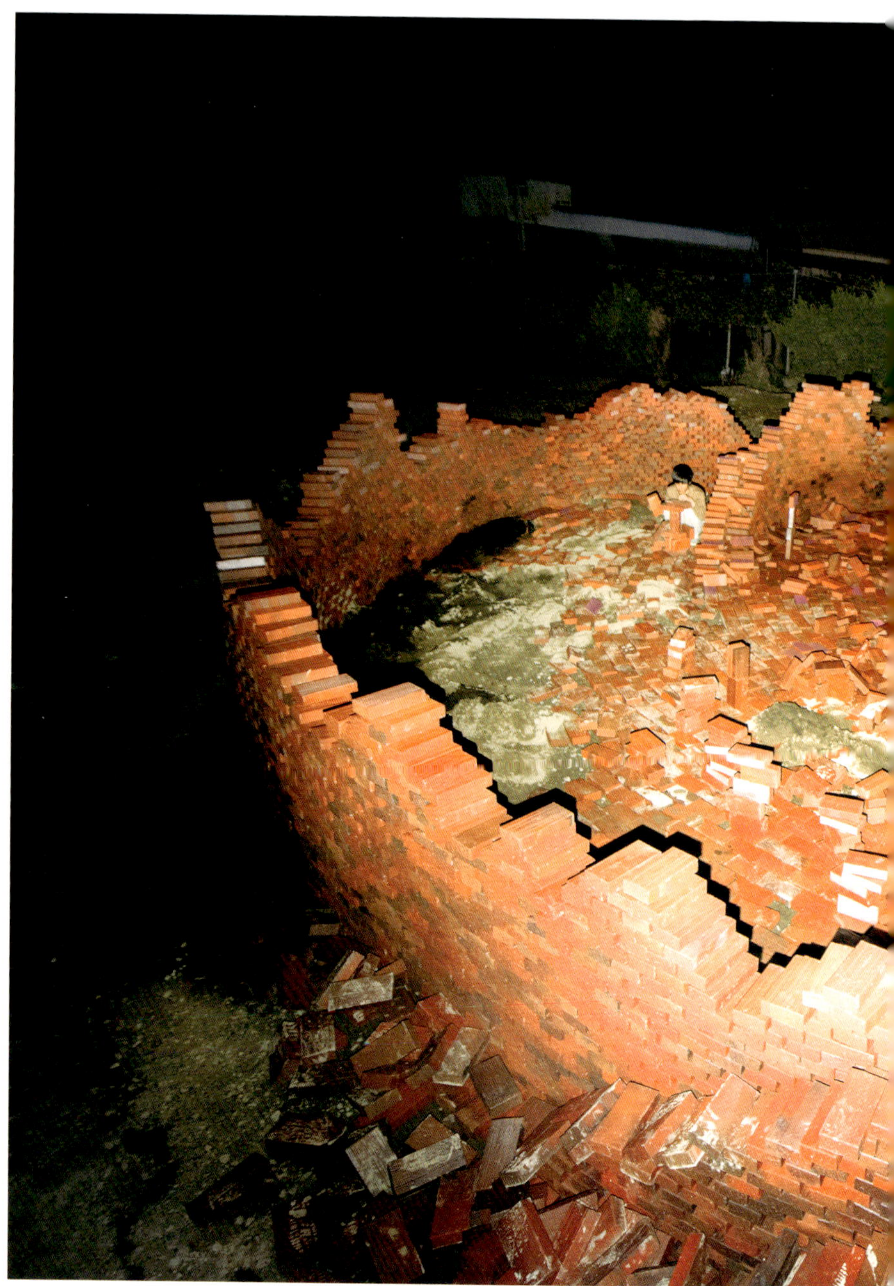

 Breaking down from the inside 2018 (*Human Spring* series)

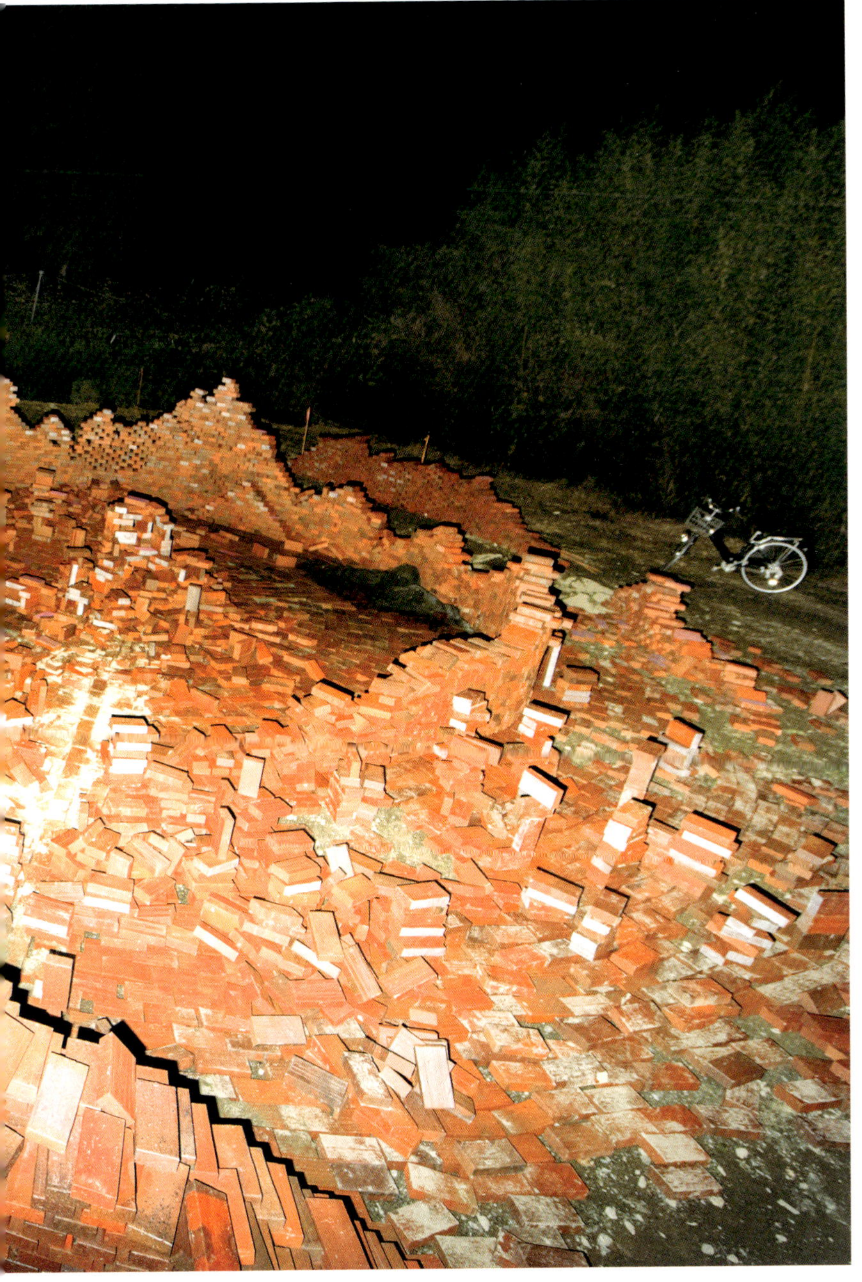

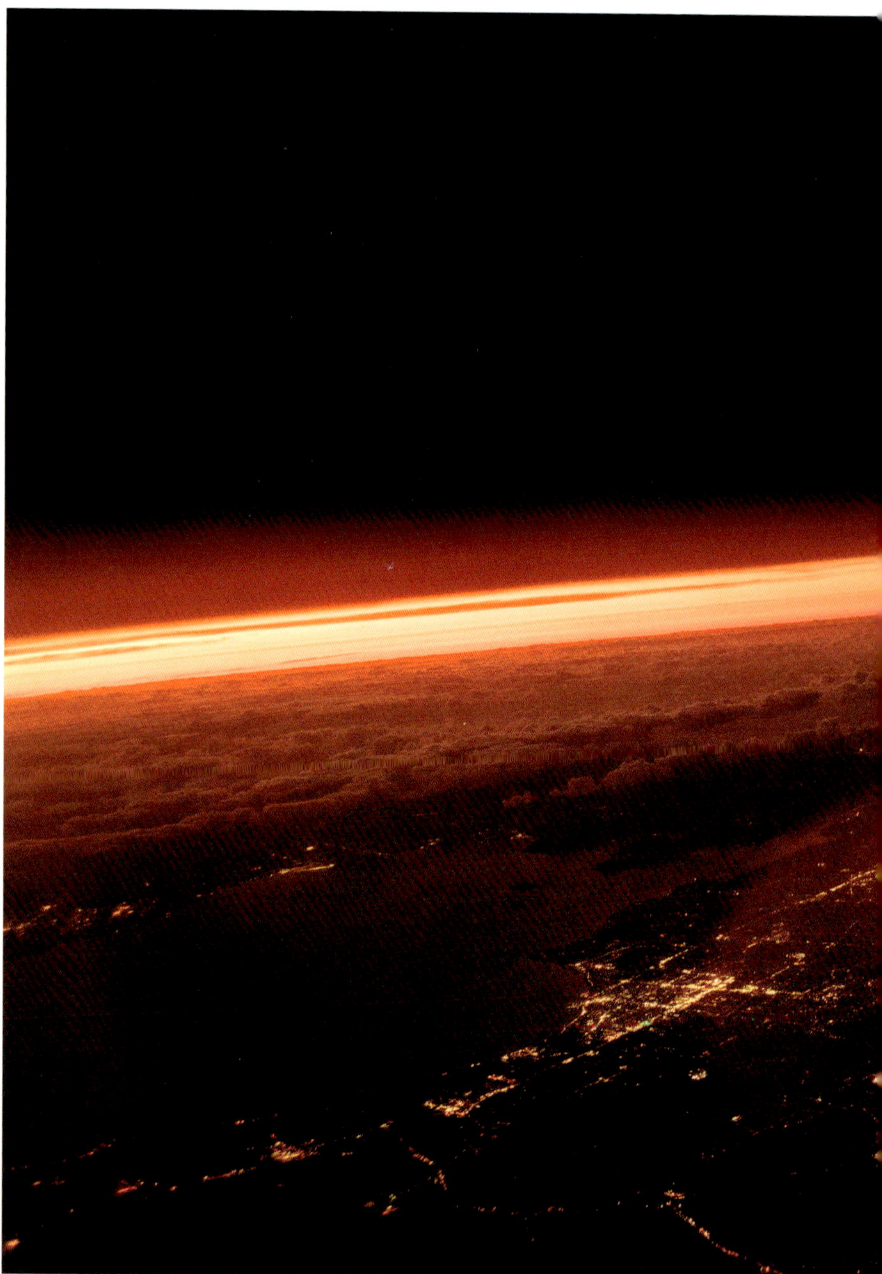

 To die while living 2019 (*Human Spring* series)

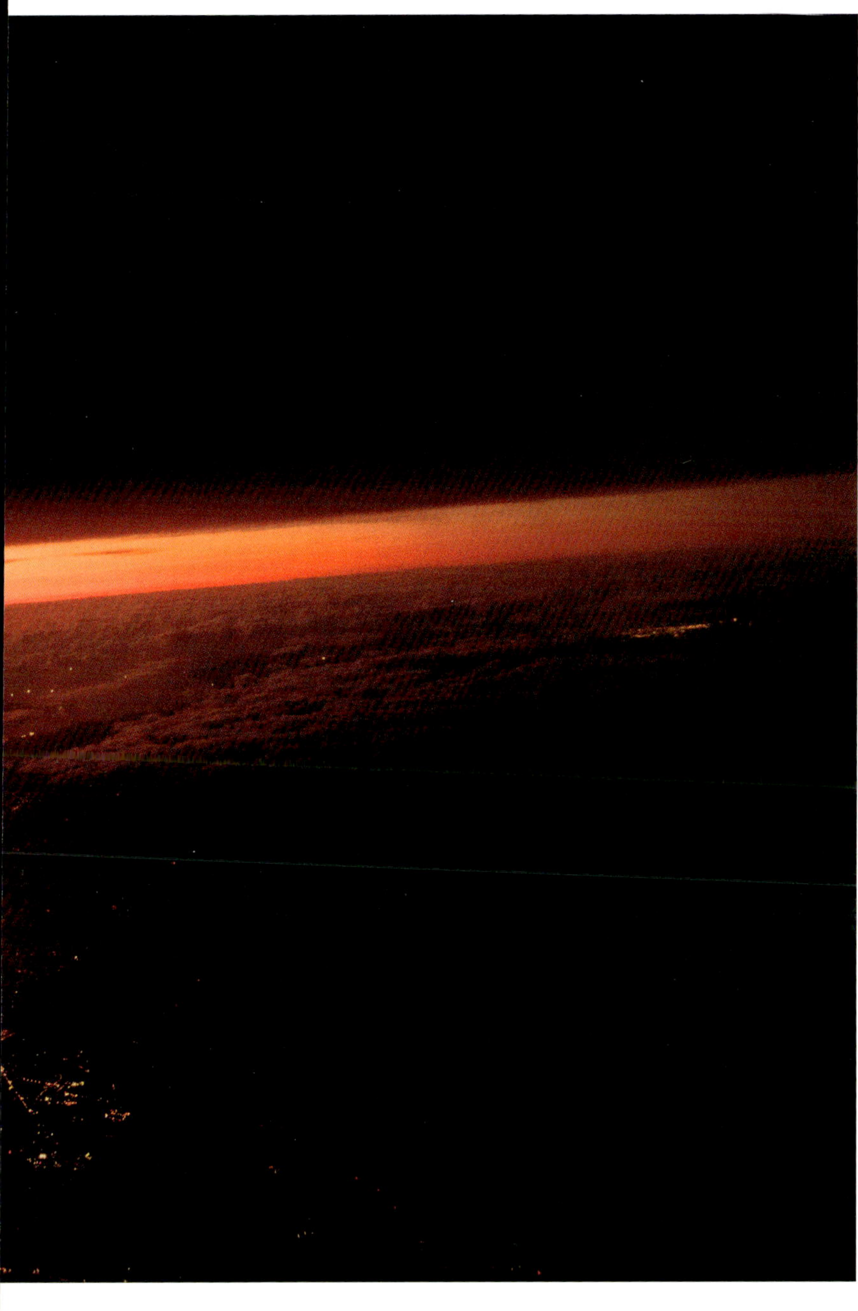

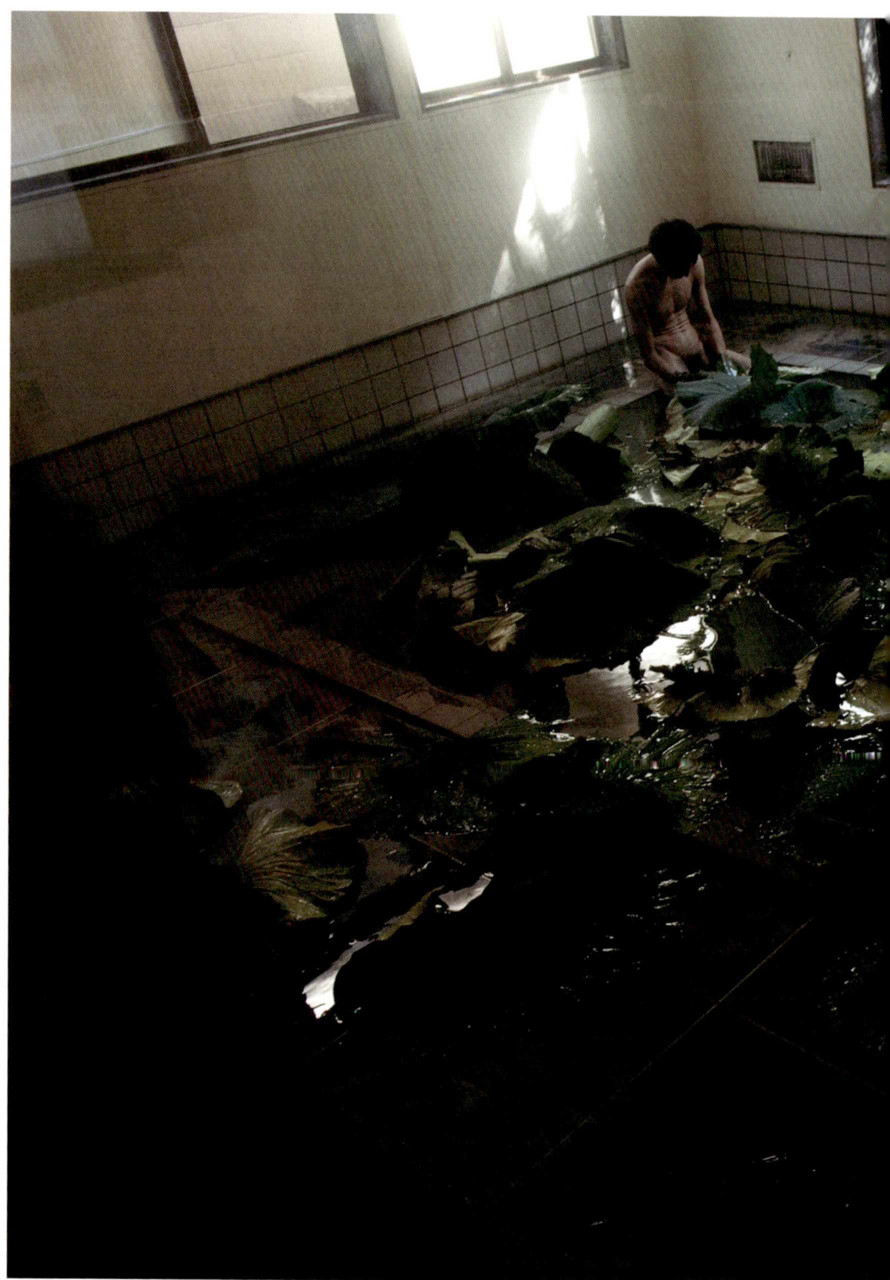

 Fujishima hot springs 2015 (*Blind Date* series)

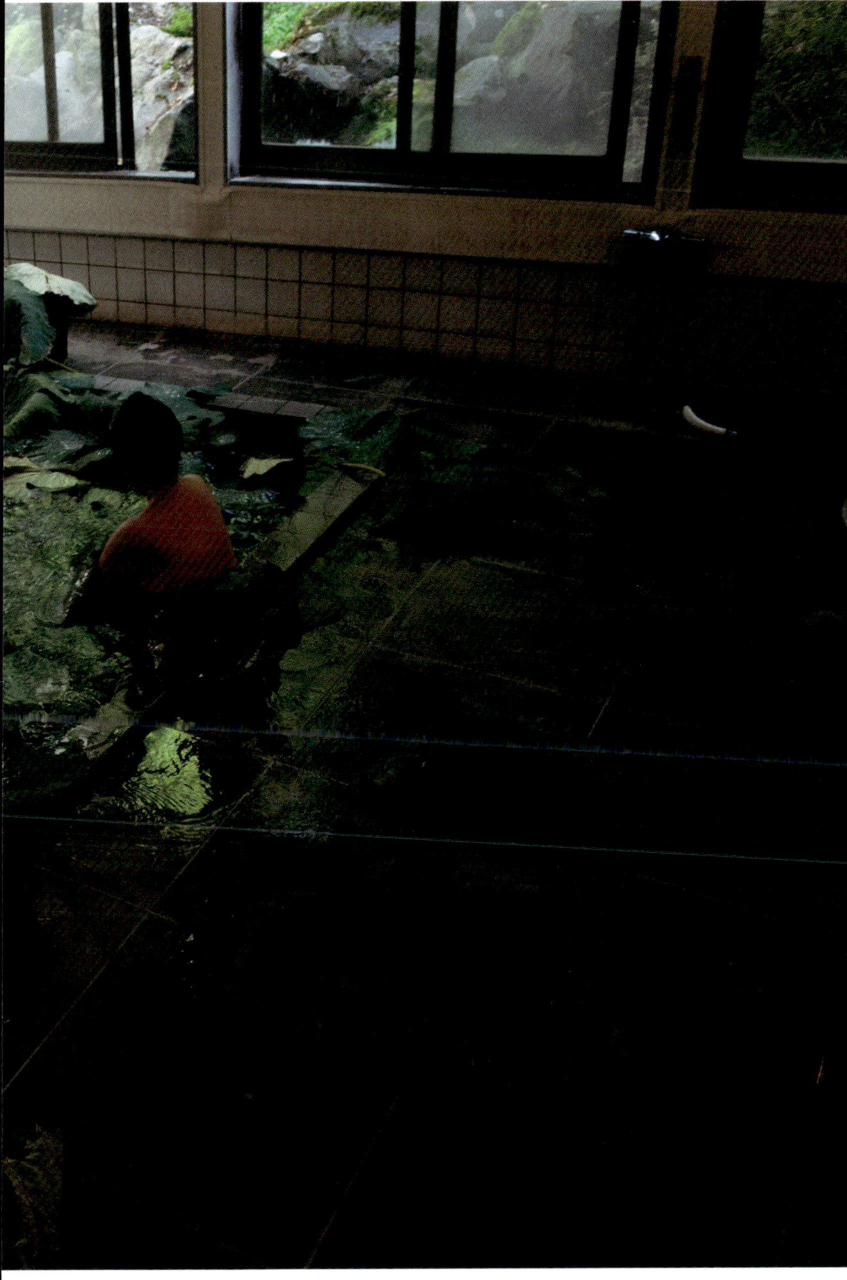

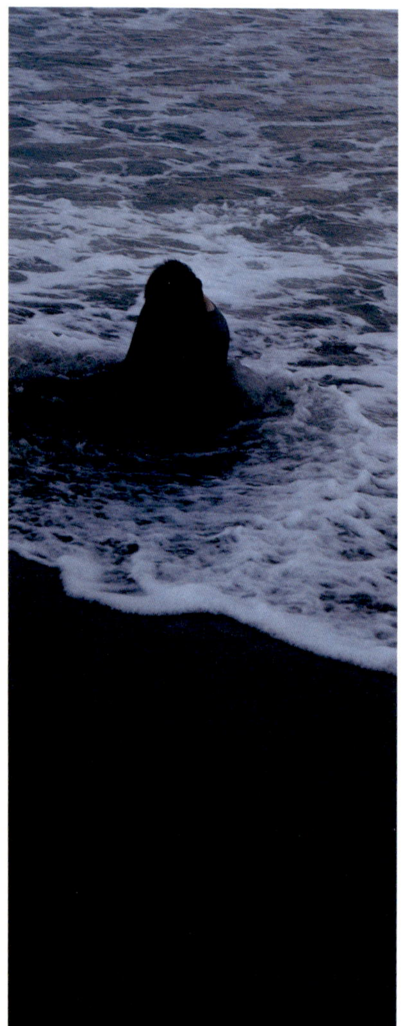

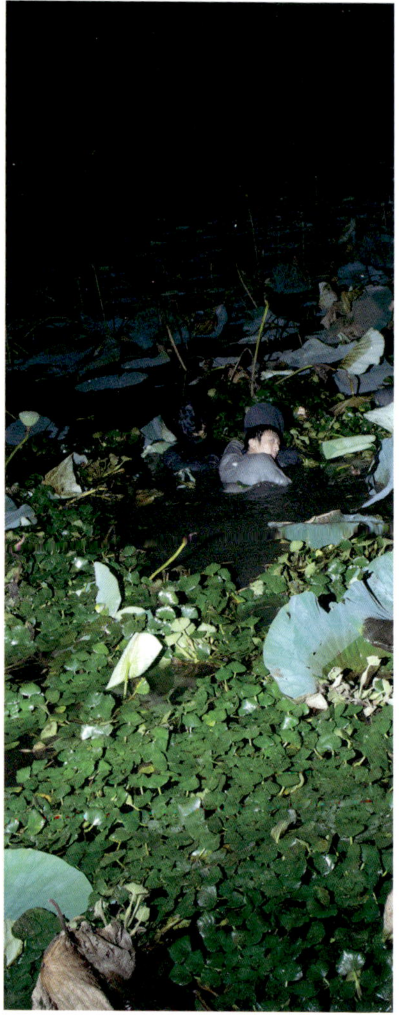

Me within a mirror 2019
Don't let your eyes meet, if you do, they will definitely come to you 2019
(*Human Spring* series)

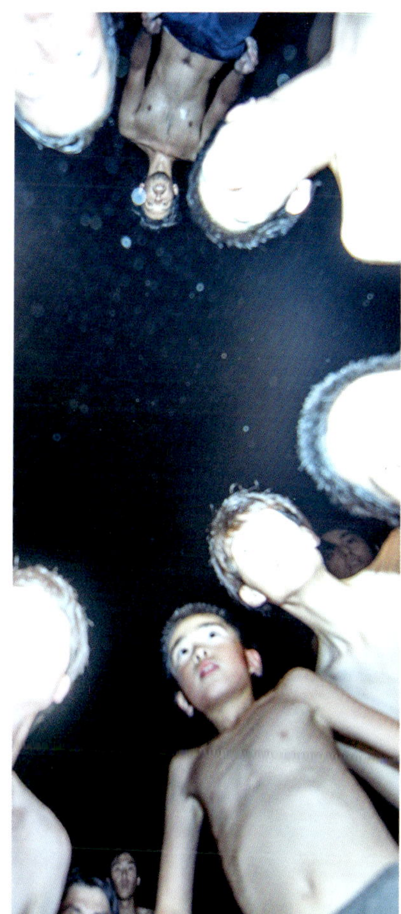

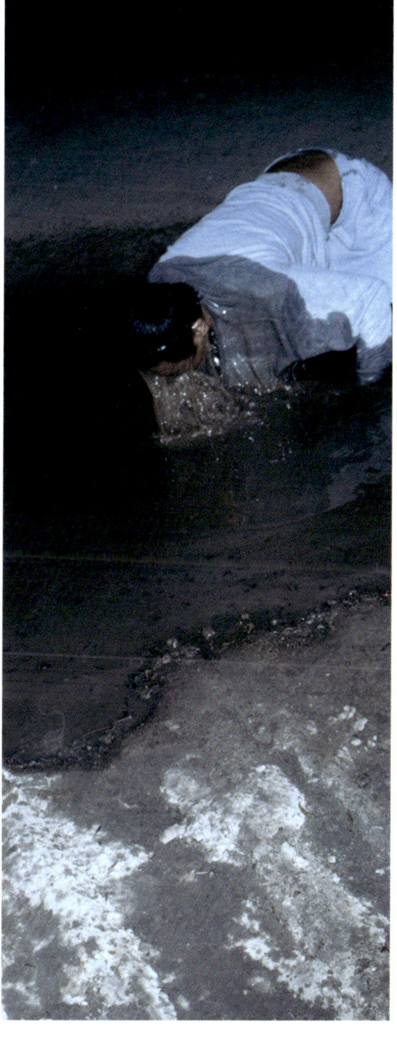

Don't let your eyes meet, if you do, they will definitely come to you 2019
Me within a mirror 2019
(*Human Spring* series)

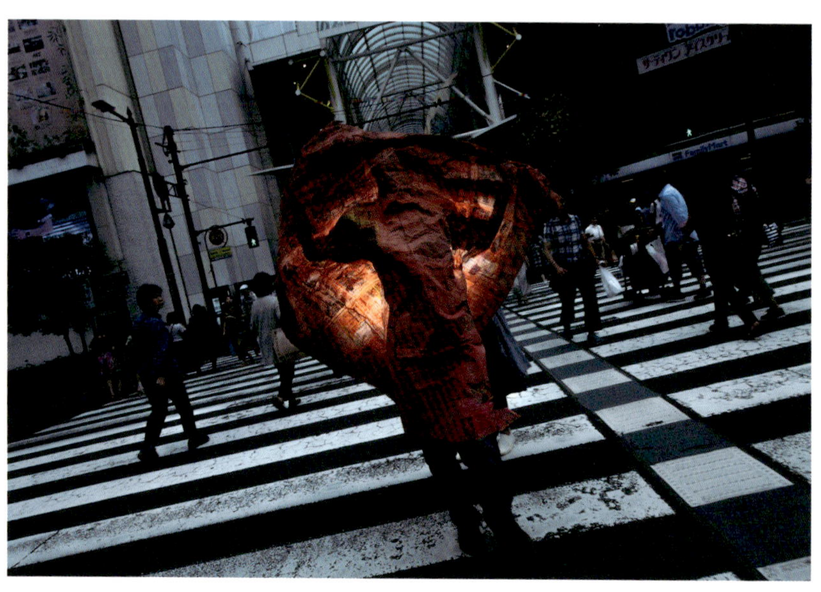

Today is the same as yesterday; tomorrow will be the same as today 2018
(*Human Spring* series)

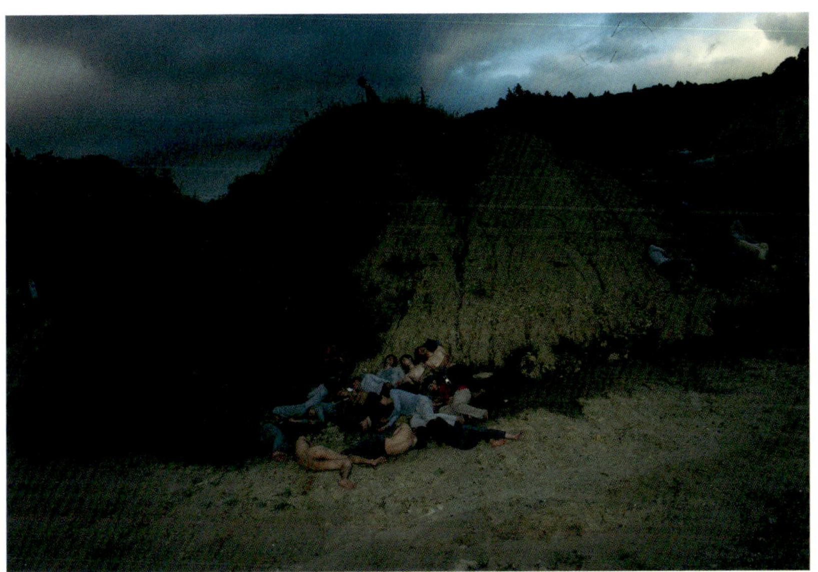

 'Mourning – Was somebody awake?' 2017 (*Human Spring* series)

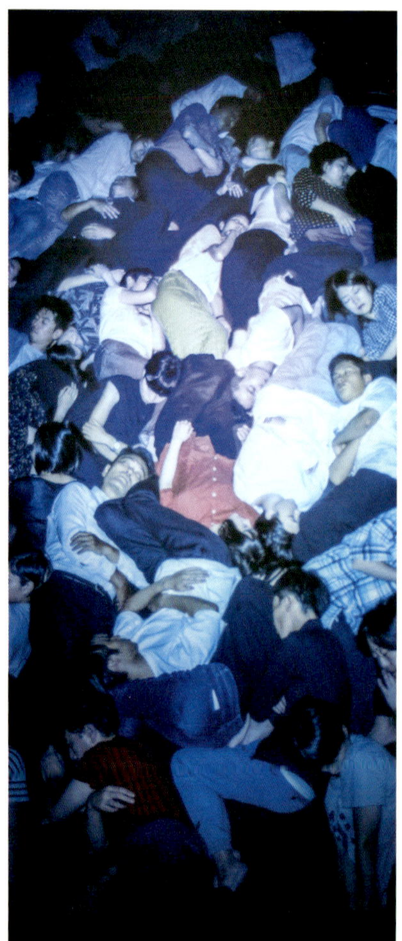

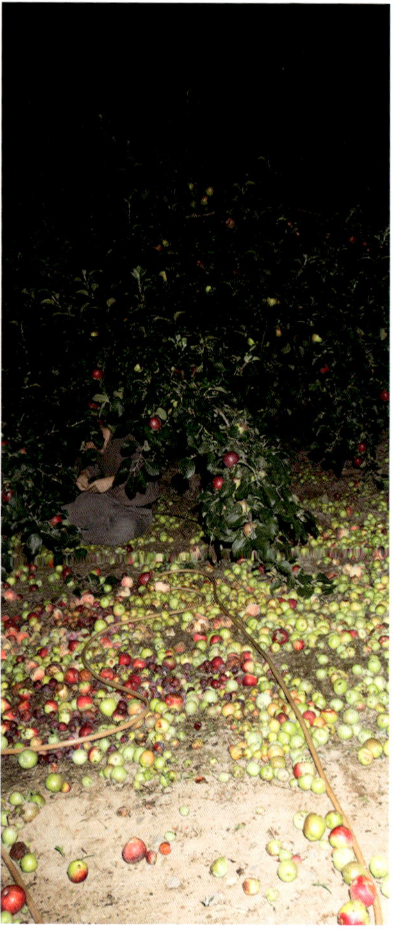

Me within a mirror 2019
Don't let your eyes meet, if you do, they will definitely come to you 2019
(*Human Spring* series)

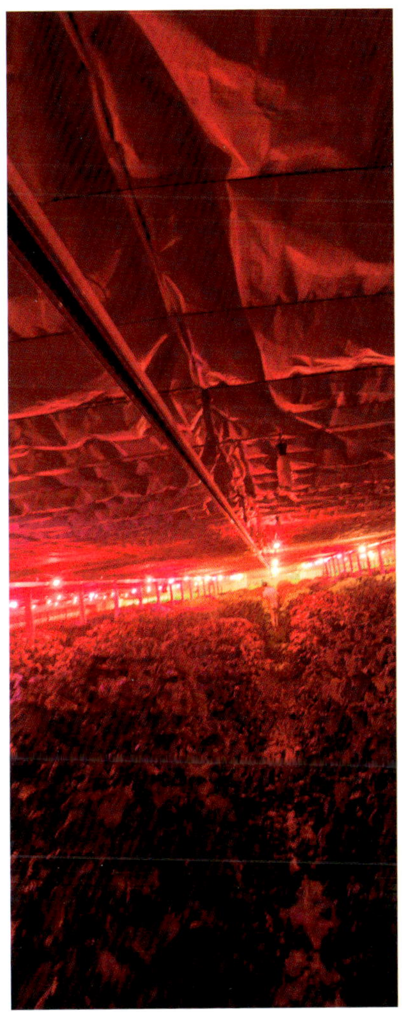

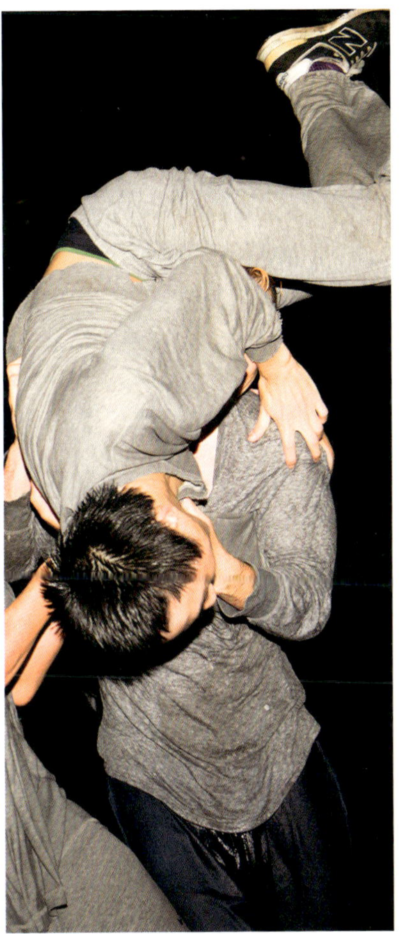

Silent Spring 2018
Zero gravity 2019
(*Human Spring* series)

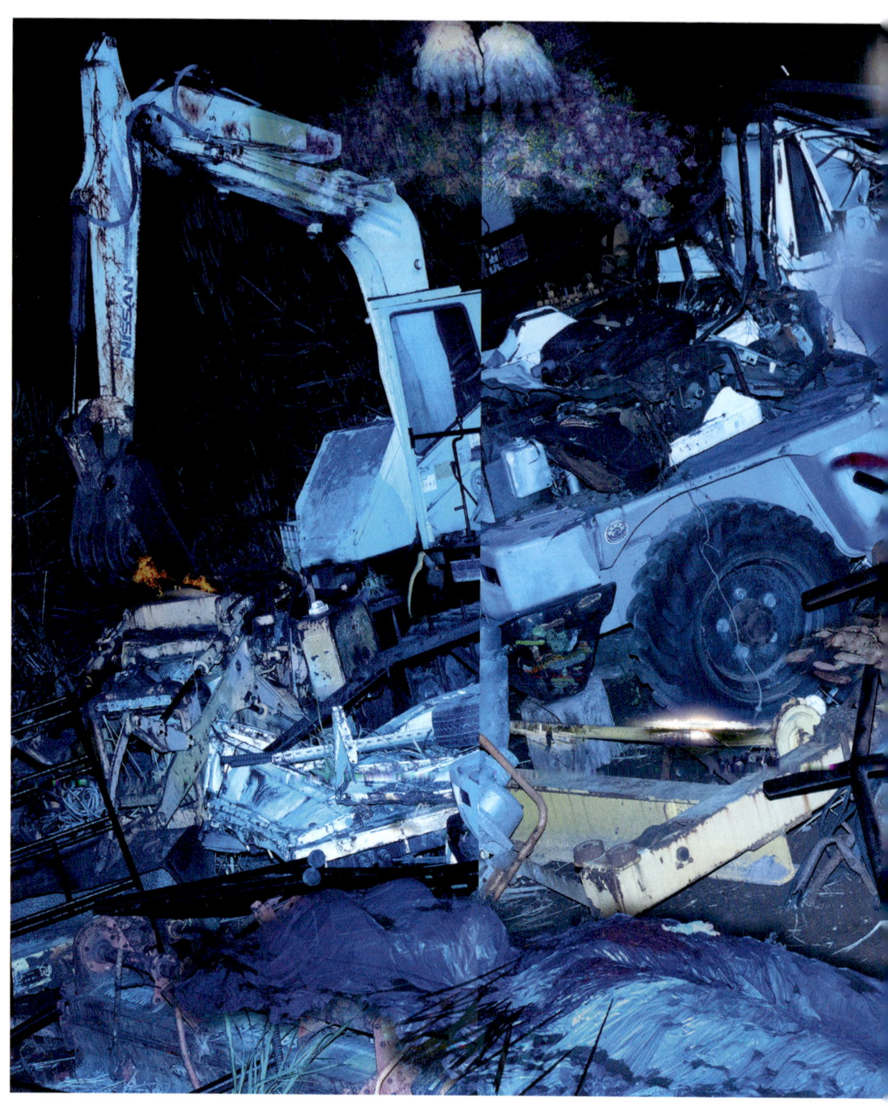

Where that night leads 1/5 2023

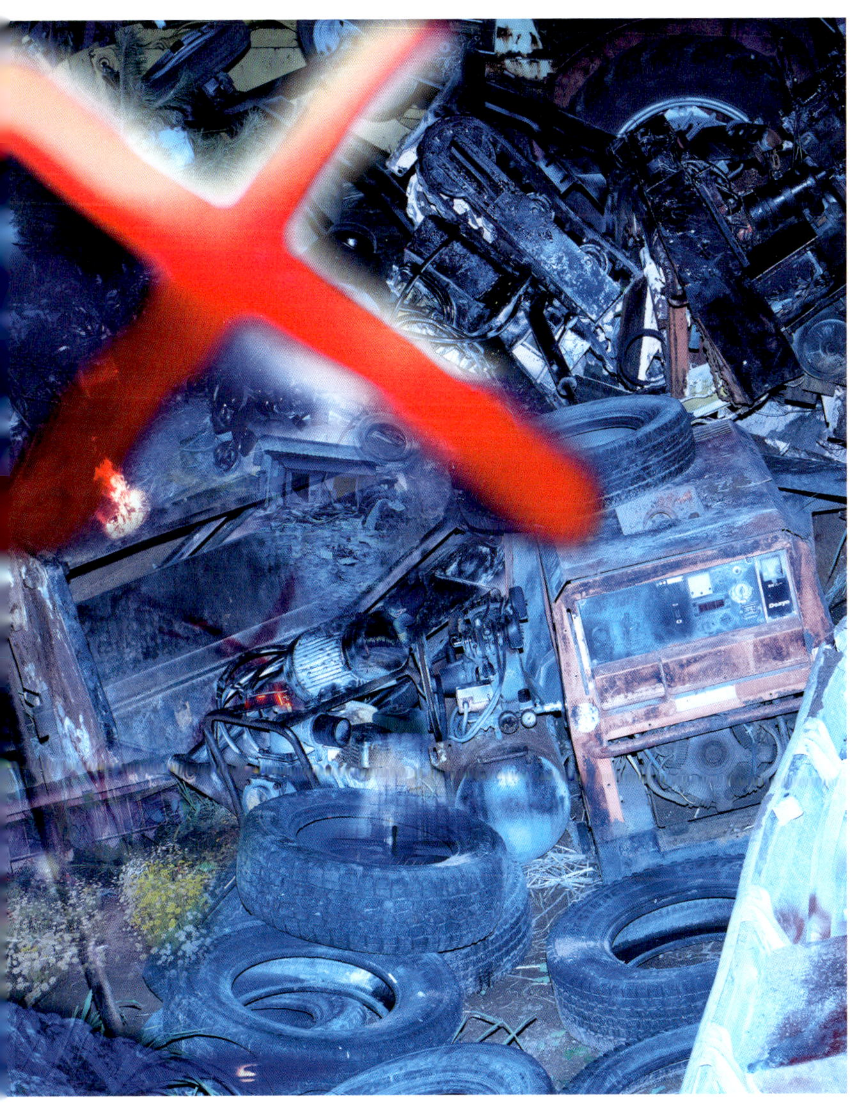

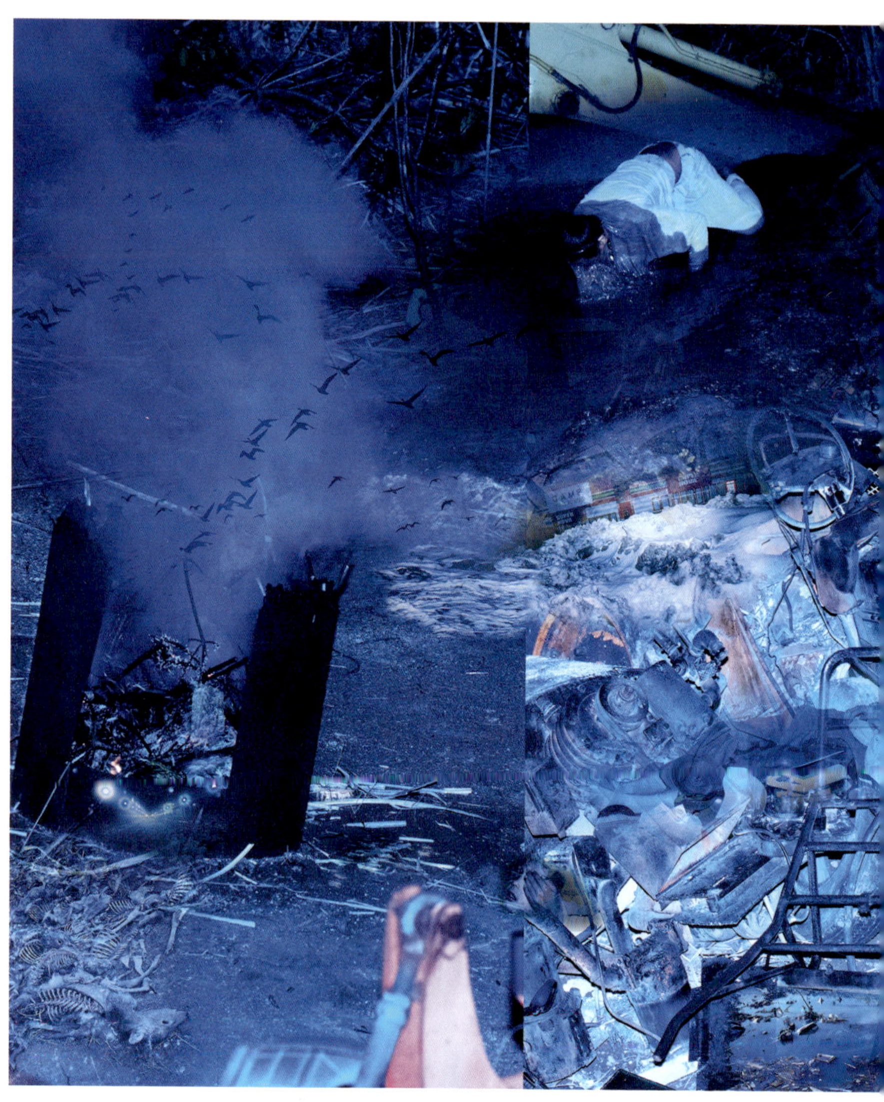

Where that night leads 2/5 2023)

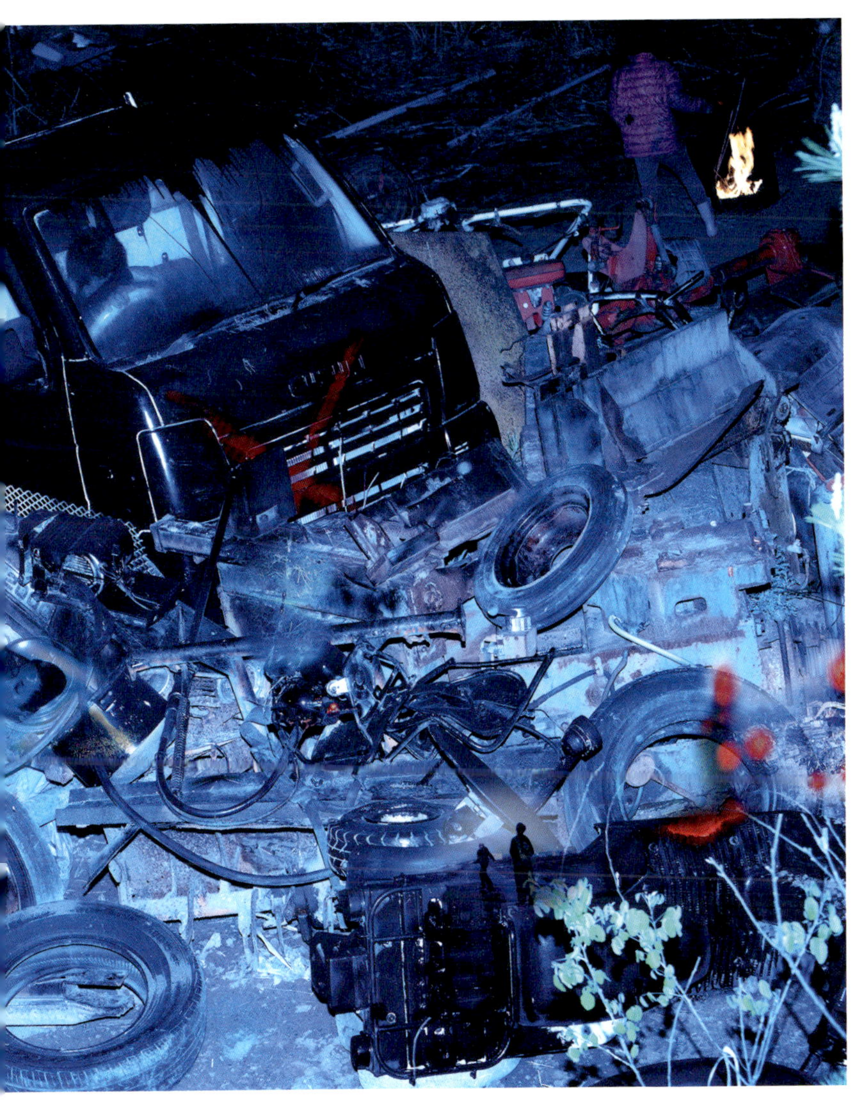

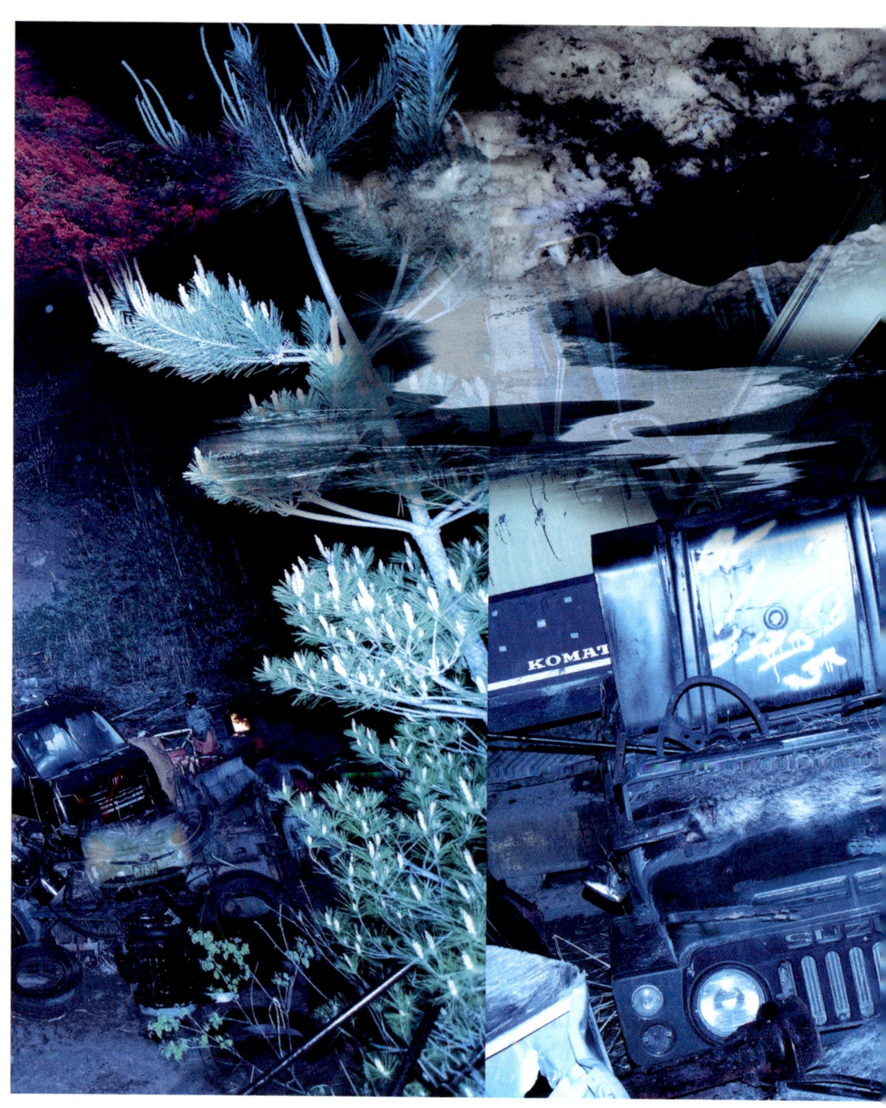

     Where that night leads 3/5 2023

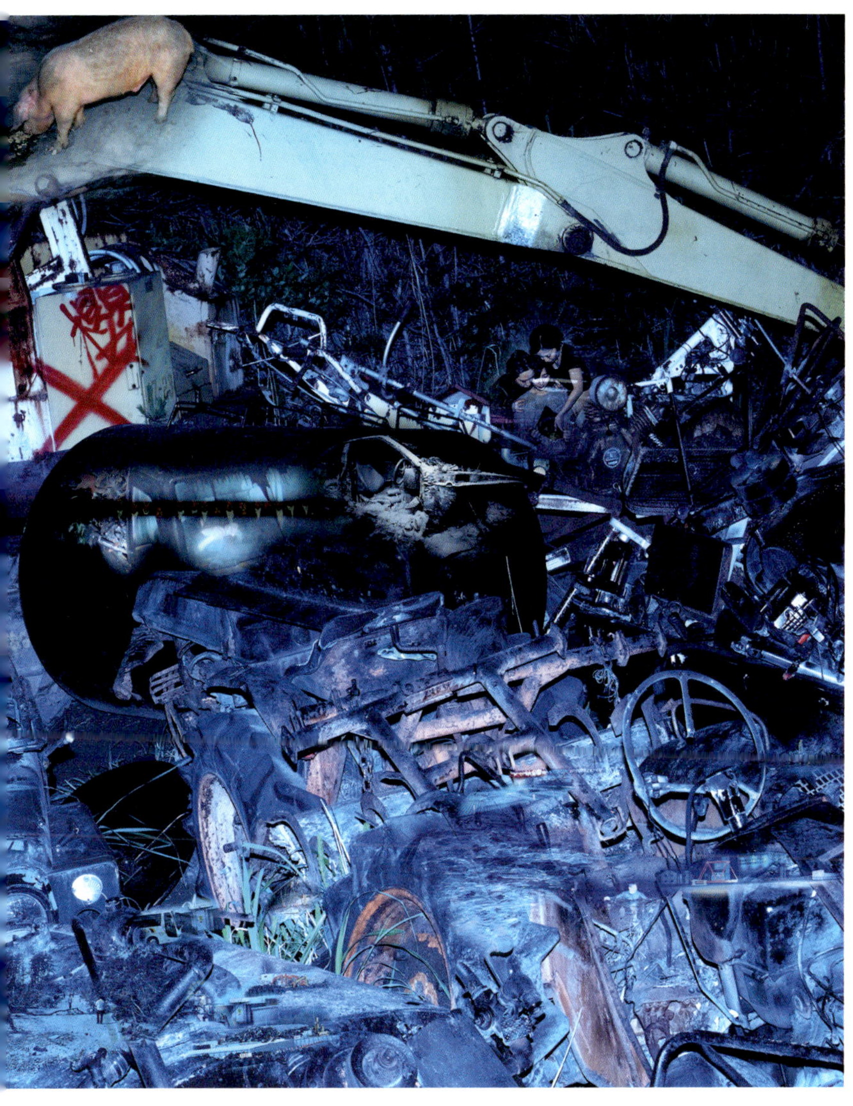

ARTIST'S ACKNOWLEDGEMENTS

Yuta Segawa

Kazuhiro Shiga
Yoshiko Shiga
Tamotsu Shiga
Michiko Kasahara
Shigeki Hattori
Ashley Rawlings
Hideki Toyoshima
Hiromi Tango
Dominique Klevinghaus
Satoko Kako
Alcuin Stevenson
Chiako Kudo
Makoto Nakahara
Shihoko Iida
Masashi Kohara
Yoshinori Kobayashi
Yusuke Kurihara
Shiita Segawa
Yutaka Ito
Mitsuko Ito
Hosoya Syuuhei
Kent Shimizu
Chinatsu Shimizu
Yoshitomo Nagasaki
Sotaro Kikuchi
Takahiro Sato
Goto Yuto
Nozomu Onodera
Osamu Sakurai
Rina Sakurai
Amanda Maddox
Ashley Rawlings
Dai Chiba
Naoko Kikuchi
Hiroko Saito
Misato Fukuda
Tomoki Abe
Daishiro Mori
Mariko Takeuchi
Maho Masuzaki
Yuki Nakamura
Michiko Umemura

Residents of Kitakama village
The Arimura Family
The Oikawa Family
The Segawa Family
The Kurihara Family

Contact Gonzo
Hyslom hysteresis
PUMPQUAKES

Ishidou Construction Co .Ltd.
Color Science Labo Co. Ltd.

Sendai Mediateque
Tokyo Photographic Art Museum
Tokyo Arts and Space
Museum of Contemporary art Tokyo

AKAAKA ART PUBLISHING
T&M Projects

CREDITS

All artworks © Lieko Shiga